M000237564

DELIVERED

BUT

DAMAGED

II

Dr. Charles E. Rodgers

Delivered But Damaged II

Copyright © 2017
Dr. Charles E. Rodgers

All rights reserved. Printed in the United States of America. No part of this book may be used or reproduced in any manner whatsoever without written permission except in the case of brief quotations in critical articles or reviews.

For more information contact:

Typesetting, Book Layout and Editing by
Enger Lanier Taylor for In Due Season Publishing

Book Cover: Lerico Britton Designs

Published By: In Due Season Publishing
             Huntsville, Alabama
             www.indueseasonpublishing.com
             indueseasonpublishing@gmail.com

ISBN-13: 978-0-9992387-0-7
ISBN-10: 0999238701

Contents

Acknowledgments

There are many people who have made significant investments in my life and the process that formed this book. First, God has allowed me the grace to find a relationship with Him and tolerated me through the process of learning how to live godly and my committing to His will.

I am grateful for my wife Carlett for being my partner, my friend, and the love of my life. Her unselfish mannerism and spirit has allowed me to be who I am and freed me to become what our God has said.

Thanks to my mother (Dorothy Rodgers), who is now deceased. She was my greatest support since early ministry. Without her belief in me, I could not have made it to this point.

Thanks to my church family for allowing me to serve you and for your support during my endeavors while the writing this book.

Introduction

I have been overcome with the discovery about both the grace that delivered me from the "world" and how much damage came to me on my way to grace. I was and in many ways, I am a mess. However, that is what makes the born again experience so much more gracious and powerful that I could have ever imagined. Now I have a voice that is not just filled with sound bites or platitudes that the church uses to sanitize this journey to faith, but the blood of my victories and my failures. There have been discouraging moments and disappointing seasons, where I not only let down others, but myself. This has been quite a journey and what I know now is that it is not unlike anyone else's journey. We are all men of like passions and we share in the totality of events that can be both fulfilling and surprising. Surprising because over the years I have been in stages where I've overcome in one season and seemed to be fighting the same fights in others. Victories are not always final. Don't make the mistake of thinking that your lust can go unchecked. Like any addict, you must be aware of the triggers or you will find yourself back in the same place you left again. Bound again to the same taskmaster and starting from a place that you felt that you had long overcome.

It amazes me how a perfect God took an imperfect me and created situations and circumstances that seemed like they were designed to defeat me, but they actually matured me. This is where what Paul said makes sense in Romans 8:28, "And we know that all things work together for good to them that love God, to them who are the called according to His purpose". As a young believer I found myself continually frustrated in my faith walk and in my pursuit of perfection. I continued running into those imperfections daily and often confused by how impossible it seemed to meet the expectations of the church, myself, and people who themselves could not meet those very expectations. Let me be clear, because I am fully aware that a life surrendered to God has to include a lifestyle of godlikeness, and part of the evidence of that godlikeness is seen in your willingness to submit your appetites to His will. This is critical and has to be said first because we live in a time where the church defines grace as a license to gratify the flesh and we are quickly drifting from the revealed mandates of God into a kind of self-defined brand of Christianity more palatable to the masses.

Who can argue that more and more Christian churches, denominational, and independent so called Christian bodies have responded to the pressure of maintaining massive cathedrals, and elevated budgets and huge congregations by rebranding the message of a godlike lifestyle to a more trendy self-improvement message that requires little more than you becoming a better person through success (often financial) in life.

This kind of shift has endangered the idea of separation between the holy and unholy in the church and the world. Today, new believers are rarely confronted with the message of personal responsibility and surrender that I had to face "in the old days" as a young believer in the San Joaquin Valley town of Merced California in 1979. We were taught that it was just as important to live in a way that proved that you are saved from the appetites of the world, that it was to be saved from the world. To be saved in those days meant that you conformed to the commands of the scriptures and the rules of the church; no matter how grievous. Most of the messages that were delivered from the pulpit dealt with the issue of separation from the world and living apart from "sin." The Old Testament addressed this issue by speaking of the clean and unclean. An unclean person had to avoid that which was unholy and take steps to return to a state of cleanness before returning to worship. The failure to do so placed them in danger of a divine retribution. In Leviticus 15:31, *"You must keep the Israelites separate from things that make them unclean, so they will not die in their uncleanness for defiling my dwelling place, which is among them."* They also had to go through a ritual of purification in order to return to a place of cleanliness. Purification always involved a waiting period and sometimes involved washing or atoning sacrifices. The central reason for this system was to remind them that not only is God holy, but that man is contaminated.

In the New Testament, "unclean" was used in more of a moral sense rather than a ritualistic sense. Jesus emphasized that it wasn't as important to avoid certain physical items as it was to clean your heart and mind of the filth that can be found in them. Jesus never hesitated to touch lepers, sinners or the dead and He even allowed them to touch Him. They never contaminated Him; but on the contrary, He cleansed them. In Mark 7, when the Pharisees asked Jesus why the disciples ate bread with unwashed hands, Jesus gives them a dialogue and later explained it to His disciples in verses 18-20, *"Are ye so without understanding also? Do ye not perceive, that whatsoever thing from without entereth into a man, it cannot defile him; because it entered not into his heart, but into the belly, and goeth out into the draught, purging all meats. And he said, that which cometh out of the man, that defileth the man."*

This theme of separation of the heart is not as prominent in our churches anymore, nor is it often seen. Separation has been replaced with integration in an effort to demonstrate that we can incorporate Christianity into the world. We justify all this by saying we have become relevant. However, in gaining relevance we have lost much of our influence and we have surrendered our power. The result of all of this is that we have dumbed-down and streamlined personal responsibility so that no one will be left behind. As a consequence, it has resulted in there being very little difference between those in the church and those in the world. Nevertheless, the word of God remains valid and none of us has a pay grade high enough to change it. In 1 Kings 2:3 it says, *"And keep the charge of the Lord your God; to walk in His ways, to keep His statutes, His commandments, His judgments, and His testimonies, as it is written in the Law of Moses."* Now we have to believe first that the Bible is the absolute map that tells us how to get to the will of God. If that is the case, then our primary goal is to walk in God's ways, keep His statues, commandments, and judgments. Nothing that happens on this earth or in the passage of time can change what God has already spoken in His word. So the teachings about holy lifestyles are confirmed in scripture and cannot be abdicated.

I've understood this since my childhood, without knowing any passages of proof, but the reality of that has not removed my inner struggle and the conflict between what I want for me and what was God's perfect will for me. Therefore, as I attempt to add to the conversation through this book it would be crazy for me not to improve, and allow both sides to speak. Though my personal testimony remains, my personal assessments, as well as the damage I have experienced within the church is fluid. I understand that my assessment can't totally be based on emotion, but on systematic accounting of the biblical evidence and scholarly research. This will not rise to the standard I felt was necessary when writing my past offering, but I think it is only fair to deal with the tension of the issues presented and not just my insights and personal experiences.

Hopefully, each one of us have been privileged to experience deliverance from the destruction of sin, and if you have, don't be surprised that you may be in some wrestling matches with what you thought you had defeated. It is natural for every man to know the spiritual battle that will engage him all of his life. Though his call to godliness is real, his fight with his natural tendency is also real. Like Jacob in Genesis 32, we are in our own personal wrestling match against our will and if we are going to be found pleasing to God we must come out of the fight touched and changed by God. Consider the story of Jacob's life; he was born as a result of a prayer from his mother, a barren woman named Rebekah. Although he was the answer to a prayer he wasn't always what she prayed for; because we often ask God for the end of a thing without knowing the cost of having it. She thought that having a son would be the end of her struggle. She didn't understand that she was producing struggle; the thing that you think will bless you can become a source of problems for you. In Genesis 26, we find her pregnant with twins which were supposed to be a blessing but it was a difficult birth. Instead of being peaceful it was burdensome and while she was still pregnant, verse 22 said, *"And the children struggled together within her; and she said, If it be so, why am I thus?"* In other words, if this is the answer to my problem, why am I having all of these issues? Many of you can attest to that in your own lives. Even though you may be blessed, it is not without some unexplained issues. This is a text worthy to be considered because what Rebekah was actually saying was, "Why doesn't my life match my promise?" God promised that she would produce, but now she is in a struggle and having a hard time understanding the pains in her body. She now questions if what was growing inside of her was indeed God's blessing for her. I can tell you that the blessings of

God will sometimes be with conflicting signals. You can be encouraged that despite the ominous signs, your struggle will not stop the promise. In fact, her struggle was a sign that she was pregnant with twins. If this were a sermon, I would tell you, "Out of your struggle God is giving you double."

After Rebekah had the children, she names them. This is critical because what you call something speaks volumes about how you see it. I know this is not going to go over well with many readers. However, you must start looking harder at what you are seeing in your life, so that you won't mistake or misname the blessings that God gives. Don't forget the times when God sustained you in your famine, and produced when you were barren. Often, those things that you considered to be a problem were the forerunner to the promise. Many times I found myself in situations that threatened my reputation or my relationship with God. Poor choices, horrible mistakes, insincere confessions, and ignored carnality were my real problem.

Like most believers, I desired to please God. I was angered by people who confronted me instead of simply understanding me. I didn't realize it at the time, but they had every right to name me because it is what they saw in me. I refused to admit it, but the truth is they didn't award me my name, I earned the name. What they were calling me was a result of what I was displaying and I had no right to be angry when I had no desire to be changed. Jacob decided to run from what he refused to confront and I guess for too many years I was Jacob because instead of having the inevitable wrestling match with myself, I chose to find places where I didn't have to confront myself.

These two boys were named by their mother. She named them on how she saw them at the time, and without regard to what God said about them. You should be careful what you are naming your condition. She called her first son Esau or "hairy" and the second one Jacob, which means "cheater" or "supplanter." There is a spiritual principle that says the parents will name the children and whatever they called them is how they see them or the circumstances by which they had them. Sometimes it was not even you that named you, but the thing that somebody else experienced. They named you from their experience. What Rebekah called Jacob set the course of his life, and what people call you is the best indicator of how they see you and what they expect out of you. Jesus said to His disciples, who do men say that I, the Son of Man am? In other words, how do they see me? One can't help but think of how Jacob lived all those years knowing that people saw him as a trickster, and I'm sure that they responded to him based on how they saw him. Who would have wanted to be called cheater, liar, killer, or so forth? However, the major problem I have with Jacob is that instead of believing God for his destiny, he spent his life becoming what was expected by those who named him. You should be careful what you call things in your life and what you allow people to call you.

All through the lives of these brothers there was a struggle between them. Even before their birth, until the day they entered into a battle for the blessing. Esau was first to be born and by right was to be first in line for the blessing of their father Isaac. From the day of their birth in Genesis 26:26 we are told, *"And after that came his brother out, and his hand took hold of Esau's heel ..."* We see this pattern throughout their lives of Jacob being on the heel of Esau. But Esau never understood the value of being in position for the blessing, much like many believers today. They take what has been promised for granted and willingly trade that which is precious to satisfy an immediate hunger or thirst. In Esau's haste to be satisfied, he traded what was valuable for that which had no lasting value. Consequently, he lost what he had. It is often the case that men really never miss what has been surrendered until it is gone.

As for Jacob, he went through life thinking that he had to outwit and play schemes in order to get what he thought he wouldn't obtain. If you have to push yourself forward and use political games to be "somebody" and be known by people who still don't respect you, then it's not your time. Whatever you are chasing after is probably not for you. Whatever God has for you, He knows how to get it to you, without being assisted by you. The reason we fight to gain what belongs to others is because we don't believe God has greater for us. God had already spoken to Rebekah and said that Jacob was going to get the birthright. This means that he was fighting for something that was already his. He was so persuaded by what was supposed to happen in the natural that he never stopped to consider that God is the God of the supernatural. The time came when Jacob had to deal with himself. Not unlike most of us, who will come to that place in our lives where we have to confront ourselves and deal with our reputation and the names that we've allowed to stick to us. There may be issues that have separated and divided us from family, friends, and the church, all so we can live within the expectation of God's purpose over our lives and not our own appetite. What is rarely seen in this story is the fact that they both succumb to their appetites. Esau was so hungry to fulfill his natural appetite for immediate gratification, which was evident by his willingness to give up his birthright and miss his blessing. Jacob was drunk from the appetite of status and position to the point that he was willing to violate the brotherly bond and step over whoever he had to in order to fulfill his need to be somebody. So, they both had issues that needed to be confronted. The bible said, "And Jacob was left alone. And there he wrestled with a man all night."

I am convinced that each of us will one day have our own long night of struggle that will bring us to change. This is when we get tired of struggling with what we know we should get rid of and fight our way to change. One of the things I found out in my life and I pray that you discover in yours is that you will never meet the condition of being fully used by God until you reach a place called *surrender*. The real wrestling match was over Jacob's "surrender." After being left alone, he had to confront his past and perhaps not liking what he saw, he went through a night of transformation. All of us should have our night of transformation. There is often a cost because when the man saw that he could not prevail against him, or make him go back to the way he was living. That is when he touched the hollow of Jacob's thigh and caused it to be out of joint. The real revelation is that the real presence of God should leave you disabled from doing things by your own strength. The touch from the servant of God left Jacob unable to wrestle with God any longer. Sometimes the best thing that happens to any of us is that we were forced to surrender. The real fight with sin and our will is enhanced and strengthened by our unwillingness to surrender. While we are praying that God might take sin from us, the touch of God will render us helpless and cause us to no longer be willing to follow what we thought we couldn't let go of. My testimony of change is that after years of trying to avoid sin, all I had to do was to have a confrontation with myself over the lack of surrender that made me chase after sin and kill it. Kill it; He touched him and left his hip out of joint. Wow! God left him damaged; damaged but better. DELIVERED BUT DAMAGED. I believe that for the first time in Jacob's life he was able to really view his life and see himself differently. His confrontation resulted in him gaining an ability to see himself in light of God's love for him, and that God's love is always bigger than the "things" we get from Him. He had to be living with the knowledge of how many times his deeds and the way he treated others transgressed the law of God. During the confrontation, I believe his biggest discovery was him realizing that he was not God.

I suppose that the source of much frustration over my continued failures in life have been over my confidence in my own ability. I too have been touched, to remind me that

He is not relying on me, because I can never be Him. I'm not God, though there are times that I feel the pressure to be as perfect as God. In some ways, friends and acquaintances may remember and hold on to the details of your past transgressions and can rehearse them like they expected you to be God. What a relief to know that nobody can be God but God. In fact, there is only one who can do a good job being God, and that is God. So I'm less critical of the faults that I have and less concerned about hiding my damaged places so others won't see. I just keep reminding myself that I can't fix it, because I'm not God. My hope in this book is to demonstrate a fuller accounting of why being damaged exposed the growth of my heart. My further hope is that it is a blessing to those who read it, and life changing to those who apply the principles found in it.

Living Behind the Mask 1

One of life's great mysteries is that we all have the capacity to love, suffer, endure, and even hate. First, we are blessed with the capacity to handle more than we thought or imagined we ever could. Secondly, the knowledge of that often causes us to expose ourselves to more than we should. Who we think we are and who we would like others to see us as, seldom are the same thing. The fact that we see ourselves with great capacity is not a bad thing. Sometimes we fail to realize that along with high expectations comes additional responsibility that we are generally not ready to embrace. We are mere sinners saved by the gracious power of God, who loved us with an unexplainable love. So there aren't any works, studies, conferences, lectures, books, and positive confessions that could change the fact that our weaknesses could never be overcome by our righteousness. All too often instead of throwing up our hands and tapping out, we carry the charade of still being worthy of God's salvation. In this sense, we are no more than actors playing the part of the righteous. We have become so good at it, that we often confuse who we are with who we have been saying we are. The sad part to all of this is that often we are unhappy with our lives, but we are unwilling to confront the disappointment of our exposed truth. So we are paralyzed by the perception that others have about us and frightened by the truth we have already accepted about ourselves. Few people in the church have the courage to be themselves or to admit that there are places in their lives where they may struggle. Although we are painfully aware that none of us are perfect, we often conduct our lives as if we don't know how imperfect we really are. All of us spend a great deal of time and effort managing our issues in order to be accepted by others. Unbeknownst to us, many are managing the same issues. We are surrounded by a great cloud of witnesses on our jobs, in our schools, churches or in our neighborhoods who carry on the charade of godly consistency. In all honesty, they are men of like passion subject to the frailties offered in the world.

Few people can measure up to the image that we create for ourselves. Most of our "awe" is a result of what we imagine. The people who impress you, can do so because their deeper self has never been exposed to you. I don't want to ruin it for those of you who are star struck, but every person you meet is in some way just like the last person you met. We are all products of the dust of the ground. The bible records the great story of man's creation in the book of Genesis 1, and it always blesses me that God said, *"Let us make man in our image, after our likeness"* and in Genesis 2 we are told that *"the Lord God formed man from the dust of the ground, and breathed into his nostrils the breath of life; and man became a living soul"* (verse 7).

One cannot help but we in awe by the fact that God uses the same substances to form the beast of the field, the cattle and the birds of the air (verse 24). What distinguishes man from all of them is the fact that God breathed into his nostrils the breath of life (Genesis 2:7). We are all men of like passions who live and die. We get sick and we hunger, just like every other creature. However, the breath of God makes us unique. I hope that the criteria for impressing you is not based on what a person has or what they are able to do, because all of this will ultimately be disappointing.

What should impress us about any man is that we hold within us the breath of God. All of us are flawed and there is none who upon further examination will pass all tests. The real problem is a lack of self-awareness. It seems as though a good bit of our lives surround a quest for acceptance and conformity to the norms established by the culture around us. Gandhi once said, "Our greatness lies not so much in being able to remake the world as being able to remake ourselves. The first shock that most of us have in life is the one of self-recognition and the journey of discovering our own true self. In our infancy we became conscious of thoughts, feelings and senses. While in our twenties we may have become consumed with hobbies, friends, and fashion. In our midlife years we are typically consumed by community, faith, careers, and family. Our final years are confronted with regrets or satisfactions about our choices along the way. In some way, all of these stages eventually have led to our true self. My journey in search of my true self, didn't feel like a journey at all, but it was a test in courage and my ability to accept my contradictions, personal faults, and failures.

I can remember times when it was reinforced in my life, family and in the church that being me was unacceptable both to God and man. Nevertheless, becoming authentic can reveal things about you that you would rather people not know. There may be embarrassing, disheartening things, like a failed marriage, a child out of wedlock, rape as a child or being a rapist, history of drug abuse, struggles with homosexuality and on and on and on. The truth is that with all of your flaws, you've learned how to survive when the odds were stacked against you. There is nothing more impressive than someone who has the courage to be transparent about what they've been through. I think we should all ask ourselves how did we learn this behavior of poor self-awareness. When did I start feeling that who I am was not acceptable and start blaming people and circumstances for my maladaptive behaviors? For me I began to discover my confidence merely by letting go of my victim stories. I discovered that those stories served mostly to explain to people why I was a certain way but they did nothing to heal me of what was wrong.

In fact, it became easier to allow myself to believe that I didn't deserve the mistreatment or my struggle was not my fault. That mentality was working until one day it came to me that my circumstances were not the thing that needed changing. I needed to be changed. It was time for me to take responsibility to change my responses and behavior. However, my excuses were not changed overnight. Becoming aware of how my response to negative events was a powerful weapon in my journey of change. It empowered me with conscious choice and helped me admit my part in painful events of my past. I begin to be aware of my need for change both internally and externally. I began to understand myself, the way I was feeling; the triggers and effectively work through transforming my emotional responses. This wasn't easy because sometimes merely remembering painful history can bring back painful feelings. Again, I got rid of the victim thinking and empowered myself. I began to take note that despite what happened I did survive. Have you ever just said, "I survived?" When it could have been worse and others went through worse; but you survived. I have this new relationship with myself that is not based on others view of me. I can no longer be manipulated or emotionally abused because I give myself permission to be who I am.

The church that I pastor had a month that focused on family matters, and as a part of the family month, individual members and families were invited to come and share some aspect of their authentic self as it related to their family. I had no idea how this would turn out because one of the first rules of church etiquette is to never allow a layman to have free reign of the microphone without knowing what they are going to say, and how long it will take them to say it. But we ignored that rule this once, and people in our congregation were free to tell us about the make-up and challenges that got them to where they are. They were open to tell us about their journey. There were some incredible survivor stories from domestic violence, child abandonment and issues regarding blended families. By the time the service had closed there was a deep sense of healing all over the church as well as a great number of people who related to where they had been. The authentic self is the real self. It is the place where most people live and very seldom expose.

If you only knew what was really behind the masks that most people wear, or the curtains of secrecy they erect in their lives. The revelations of what covers them would either frighten you or encourage you. Either way you will be more thankful for what God has done for you. Just because you can't see a thing doesn't mean it does not exist. We are often surprised by situations that are revealed in others as though it is unbelievable or that it could happen to us. All of us are subject to the illusive hand of fate, and we are confronted with things we can't control and things that we won't resist. It is a part of life and none of us will get through life without some unwanted visits from "old man" trouble. Many people have become experts in disguising their struggles and secret brokenness to the degree that most people who thought they knew their real story would be surprised at how much they were able to live through.

Most of the people who we think have wonderful lives are not wonderful at all. We can only imagine their lives as wonderful because we view them with limited information. We can only envy a life that we have no knowledge of and the moment we learn the details of it, it loses all glamour. If people only knew the untold truth or stories, unrevealed pasts, the everyday burdens, internal struggles, self-doubt, and insecurities that you have endured; They would think again about wanting to be you.

To the casual observer, nearly everything about my life would be desirable, and in so many ways maybe that's true. Why God's mercy and favor stood with me, I don't know. I know that I am a perfect example that the treasures of God dwell in earthen vessels. God has been more than generous with entrusting me with His provision, protection, and insight; things that I know I don't deserve.

I'm left with the question, "Why me?" In fact, this is a question that people ask of God in times of blessings and in crisis, "Why me?"

Even the people who once knew me are often shocked over how God has chosen to frame my life. I constantly say to my friends, "God used me to confuse you." Based on merit, nobody would think that in me is housed the capacity for the Kingdom demonstration that has been exhibited in my life. No one would have picked me to be the one God uses to reflect His glory. Nevertheless, God knew everything about my life, and still chose to call me. The continued blessings that are evident on me is a real example, that God blesses who He wills, and puts up and takes down according to His own design. That doesn't eliminate the struggle, it emphasizes the power. Make no mistake, I praise God for my life of grace. But even with grace it was not without struggle. When God chose me He never said that He would eliminate all battles for me.

I have lived through some difficult circumstances;

Many of which should have left me institutionalized or even worse, dead. I know that I've been afforded this measure of grace that allows me to continue to move forward despite the things in my life that qualified me to never get ahead. The people who are casually acquainted with me have no idea about my spiritual battles nor am I aware of theirs. Each of us are trusted to stand through our own spiritual warfare and be faithful. I find that it is good to have some people exposed to the failures in your life, because it is the awareness of your weaknesses and failures that keep others from worshipping your life. If God didn't hide the real details, we would be tempted to think of ourselves more highly than we ought, but our own honest assessment should humble us and cause potential admirers to be thankful that they are not us. I'm glad that despite my best efforts, I know that my life would be considered hopeless without God's grace. I'm thankful to be able to admit that I'm guilty of breaking the law of God in too many areas to name. In fact, the only way I can still claim my love for God is through the grace given to me by God.

There have been times I would find myself feeling as though I was walking on spiritual eggshells to avoid being judged or exposed by some well-meaning believers who felt that anybody other than themselves who committed a sin was either unsaved or fake. The church is sometimes filled with spiritual lynch squads seeking the opportunity to ruin reputations and lives of those so called spiritual lawbreakers and set their lives back on course. I recall many times I nearly felt what's the use and nearly gave up; admitting that

I can never be what is expected of by people, some of who say they represented the voice of God. What's deep in all this is deep down inside I knew they were not wrong. I did feel guilty and ashamed of not rendering my deeds to God in obedience. While saying how much I loved God, so much of my life was still not totally surrendered to Him. There were times that I would ask myself, "Why is everyone able to do this but me?" In fact, when listening to most believers, they too wondered out loud why it seemed that there was such difficulty. This is where I got the concept of the mask.

I soon learned that perfection was not what I offered to God, but what God offered to me. By accepting His offer of perfection in my life, I became qualified to represent Him and follow Him even though I was still not worthy of Him. Holiness was not a perfect record. What it was closer to was a perfect heart. I had to learn to gain balance in life and close my mind to the constant pressure of rituals, judgments and perceived perfection, while learning how to live a life that honored God. As I enter into another day in my search for more revelation, I do so judging myself according to the grace of God. I began to understand that it is my responsibility to forsake things of the world. Many of my greatest struggles have not been the struggle to please God, but the fight to please the people who claim to speak for God. Some of these people had gained credibility because they were the ones who initially defined God for me. Unbeknownst to me, what some of them really did, was keep me from really knowing God at all.

Only God Knows   2

L iving a life of godliness involves facing conflict and struggle. No one who is honest with themselves can say that there are not times when their temptation doesn't overcome their resistance to avoid. The problem sometimes is that some professed Christians are not as concerned with whether there is any difference in their life as long as they are "saved." However, there are those who have a genuine desire to live a life that is pleasing to God but become discouraged when they aren't where they want to be. As mature as I consider myself to be today, my life is not totally without struggle and conflict. Our own flesh brings with it the challenge of overcoming it's desires. The Psalmist David said it best in Psalm 51:5, *"Behold, I was shaped in iniquity; and in sin did my mother conceive me."* He suggests that my nature was not taught, but that I was born with the proclivity of sinful desires that are difficult to escape. Our biggest enemy is the enemy within, which is our sinful nature, known as "the flesh." It is an inward battle of resistance that rarely subsides and is never eradicated. Just because you are saved does not mean that you have lost your sin nature. You will not lose that sin nature as long as you are in this flesh. You will always be subject to temptations, sinful desires, a battle to overcome your will, all while struggling to please God.

We are also being challenged by demonic agitations who are determined to cloud our thinking, destroy our purpose, and ruin our plans. Paul said in Ephesians 6:12, *"For we wrestle not against flesh and blood, but against principalities, against powers, against the rulers of the darkness of this world, against spiritual wickedness in high places."* This struggle is made greater by our actual desire to do what is pleasing in the sight of God, and we are constantly surrounded by this unified hierchy of devils that have been placed to fight against God's purpose in your life. This makes your efforts to yield yourself to God more difficult because we are living in a world where denying the appetites of the flesh is mostly unheard of. The path to self-denial and yielding to God is foreign to most of us, even in the church. The struggle to be in the perfect will of God doesn't always lead me to victories. There is often tension between where I am and where I should be. But despite that tension, I continue my goal to strive for the will of God.

What continues to amaze me is that God knows me and continues to love me in spite of me. Really, all of us should be extremely thankful that God knows us and loves us. We are all thankful for different things because we have all had varied experiences with God. What seems unimportant to one may be of extreme importance to someone else. The incredible gift of life that may have been visited on one person may have been demonstrated in a different way, but we should all be thankful. God may have to pull out all the bells, whistles, and prophecies of prosperity in order for you to really offer up praise. I just need to wake up and live a normal day.

For many years I have heard numerous testimonies of various kinds, such as someone being healed of cancer, high blood pressure, or someone being able to walk away from a car accident. I've also heard people thanking God for overcoming addictions, rescuing their children from some tragedy, providing jobs, houses, cars, and many other extraordinary things. I've seen people thank God for not allowing satan to ruin their day, or something as simple as blessing them with five dollars to purchase gas for their car or money to purchase a child a pair of shoes. Gratitude can be ignited by different things or shared experiences. You being able to purchase a new suit from a department store may not prompt more gratitude than someone else who was able to get theirs from a thrift store. What is normal for some can be nearly miraculous for others. Blessings can come in different forms and can only be judged by the recipient. People who have had a number of failures in their life may not need a great deal of successes to make them happy. Although, I'm careful not to get satisfied at certain places in my life, I am grateful.

One of the labels that some Christians fear the most is being called a hypocrite. The word alone implies something ominous and sinister. How dare you have the nerve to apply such a damning word to anyone. The truth is that most people who refer to someone as a hypocrite, and even those who have been labeled a hypocrite really are not clear on the definition. Strong's Greek Concordance gives us the word "hupokrites" and tells us that it is someone who is performing or acting under a mask, or a two-faced person; or someone whose profession does not match their practice; or someone who says one thing and does another. I can clearly see why no one wants to be seen as a hypocrite. Pretending is not limited to the Church of Jesus Christ. Although it is most often refers to people who are in the church. By definition, you will find people who fit this definition in every setting. Whether it is on your job, in your school, or even in your home. The claim or the pretense to hold a belief, feeling, standard, or virtue that you don't actually hold is something that most of the people I have met are guilty of.

I received my early mindset of Christ in a church where there was a real emphasis on sin-free living. Even to the point that anyone's admission of failure to live up to standards prescribed in the church were harshly criticized and many times, publicly chastised. Everyone frowned upon and were shocked by the revealing of some sin in the life of a believer.

Much of our conversation was either thanking God that we didn't commit a sin, or having discussions about the person who was found to have participated in sinful acts. Our sense of spiritual superiority when comparing our faithfulness to their failure was empowering. I know now that we were merely actors because all of us without exception, presented ourselves as keeping a standard that we actually didn't hold. We may have been successful in avoiding some behaviors but all of us were guilty of some discretion. As I see it now, we were all hypocrites by definition. Every one of us were in violation of the law, and regardless of how much of the law we were able to keep, we were guilty of what we failed to keep. The Apostle John makes it clear that *"All unrighteousness is sin"* (1 John 5:17). Everyone has sinned; believers and non-believers alike. Romans 6:23 tells us, *"All have sinned and fallen short of the glory of God."* I hope that we never forget that our status as "saints" was given to us and it is not something we earned because we have been justified by faith. We are not righteous, but because we have accepted the remedy for sin offered by Jesus Christ, when God looks at us He declares us to be righteous. We still have sin in our members but we practice holy living which no sinner can do and by that we have been placed in a category of the righteous.

A process is happening within us every day called sanctification. This is the process where the nature of Christ is causing us to become like Him more and more each day. This process would not be necessary if we were sinless or if we didn't need it. All we need do is look back at the children of Israel and you will see that none of them could claim a spiritual condition of sinlessness or of being absolutely perfect or guiltless. Furthermore, it is interesting that Paul writes to the Corinthians, *"But I discipline my body and bring it into subjection, lest, when I have preached to others, I myself should be disqualified"* If Paul was sinless there was no reason to bring his flesh into submission to the Spirit, it would already be submitted.

Now I think it is important that I address those who are still saying, *"I don't sin"* and have drawn reference already where the bible commands us not to sin. References such as *"Whosoever is born of God doth not commit sin; for His seed remaineth in him; and he cannot sin, because he is born of God (1 John 3:9).* Simply based on the previous evidence this cannot mean that we are sinless. This doctrine that is still held in many places and in some hearts of "Absolute Perfection" should not be proof that some Christians may be perfect, but it has no power unless it is saying to us that all of them are perfect. Because "whosoever is born of God doth not commit sin.." No one should be excluded and there should not be a special group of overcomers, but every born again believer would have to be separated from any act of sin; commission and omission. This verse does not tell us that it is impossible to sin as a Christian. What it does tell us is that when we are born of God, sin should no longer be a constant goal. The new nature that we have received is now at constant war against the old nature. Our desire is now to do the will of God and not our own. Like Paul stated in Romans 7, the desire to do evil is still in conflict with my new desire for good, but I war day after day not to surrender to it, because I am not born of God. Listen to this, *"but each one is tempted by our own desire and dragged away and enticed. Then, after desire has conceived, it gives birth to sin; and sin, when it is full-grown, gives birth to death."* The appetite for sin within us does not originate from the outside but from the inside. We are drawn away by our own desire. If this is true and it is, then sin is a reaction to some temptation.

We are not hypocrites, we are in process. We do not owe each other any proof. Christ is our proof of perfection and we are not saved because of what we did not do, but what we did do. We accepted the remedy for sin offered by Jesus Christ. We read these words in Galatians, *"knowing that a man is not justified by the works of the law but by faith in Jesus Christ, even we who have believed in Christ Jesus, that we might be justified by faith in Christ and not by the works of the law; for by the works of the law no flesh shall be justified. But if, while we seek to be justified by Christ, we ourselves also are found sinners."* This is a clear case presented by Paul that we are not made righteous by keeping the law but by our faith in the works of Jesus.

One of the greatest inspirations for this writing is the power of failing. Failing in my life didn't make me a failure. Failures only educated and remind me that everything doesn't always have to turn out as planned to be according to plan. There were many times I did what I knew not to do, and violated what I knew God was against. Even being armed and equipped with the knowledge of His will, I chose to step out of His will. I can recall the numerous times God provided a way of escape for me and I could have avoided sin, but failed to take what He offered and chose rather to sin. These violations often resulted in my being left guilty, confused and ashamed; but God still loved me.

Guilt and failure can keep you from exploring many opportunities of knowing the joy of living in reconciliation with God and has blocked many believers from the opportunity of knowing the deliverance of God. It is important to stop and acknowledge our failures because the scripture requires it. *"If we confess our sins, He is faithful and just to forgive us our sins, and to cleanse us from all unrighteousness"(1 John 1:9).* You must stop to acknowledge your failures, but not be paralyzed by the guilt of them which will cause you to decrease your trust in God for your future.On the other hand, when you admit that you have "missed God", it releases you to go back and find His true will for your life. The guilt of failures will cause you to question God's care for you and His commitment to your life. I don't know how many times I played it safe, or the number of real opportunities I missed because of my fear of failing. There has always been this internal debate over whether I should hold on to what I have or risk it all for what I don't have. Fear can be a real deterrent for your future. If satan can convince you of your unworthiness and point out the things that disqualify you, you will never succeed past where you are right now. This is equally true when it comes to your lifestyle with God. Fear is a real driving force to trap you into a life of diminished service. It strains your witness, and encumbers your willingness to serve.

The truth is that God uses the power of your failures to bring you to total dependence on Him. The prodigal son's decision did not disqualify him from being a son with all the rights that he had before he left his father. David's horrible string of sins didn't change God's mind about his being a man after the heart of God. Peter's predictable outburst didn't keep Jesus from bringing him into His inner circle. God used all of their failures to bring total dependency on Him. I found that my behavior often did not please Him. Yet my awareness of my shortcomings caused me to fall more heavily on the mercy of God. By accepting His offer of perfection in my life, I became qualified to represent Him and eligible to stand with Him.

I had to learn how to balance the determination to obey God with the knowledge of my own inability to measure to the awesomeness of God. By doing so, I no longer felt the constant pressure to live a life of rituals and judgment by others. As I entered into another day, I did so judging myself according to the grace of God and not others. My responsibility to forsake those things of the world soon became a privilege to do. Our greatest struggle has not been trying to please God, but the fight we endure to please the people around us, who oftentimes are the people who initially defined God for us, and kept us from really knowing Him.

He Protects His Purpose   3

I am always amazed that God never gave up on using me—no matter what anyone else felt about me. As unpredictable as I have been at times, it never threatened the love that God has had for me. Paul said in Romans 8, *"Who shall separate us from the love of Christ."* This is an interesting and often misunderstood scripture in the New Testament. Primarily because when we read it, our focus is often on our steadfastness. We often say it means that no trouble that comes against me shall separate me from Christ, but that is not the message because the real truth will cause us to admit that we can be beaten. We should thank God every day that we are still serving God and that God didn't allow more upon us than we are able to bear. In fact, there have been many believers who have similar faith as yours but didn't maintain their relationship with God. Consequently, there are situations and issues that can happen that have separated a lot of people from God. Paul's intent is to say to us that regardless of how unreliable and undependable and wayward we prove to be, it will do nothing to hinder God from loving me. Nothing about me will cause God to change His mind about me. My life has been literally covered with situations that should have left me dysfunctional and choices that should have ended my faith—but God kept using me. He went through extraordinary lengths to get me to where I am today. Only God could have sustained my mind when people felt it would have been better to leave it lost. I'm forever grateful that I survived mistakes and bad choices. I survived things that I'm sure others would have not survived.

Pharmaceutical sales are at an all-time high, but I praise God for having no contribution to those numbers. God protected my mind! My normality lies in the minds of those who see it as normal, but there is nothing normal about me. According to my lineage, I would have been looked upon as an at-risk child; I was not an overachiever, nor was I considered highly ambitious. However, deep inside I always knew that God had separated me for something that no one else could imagine. This was more than just a feeling but an overwhelming assurance that constantly encouraged me. I had a belief that I had a specific assignment that would separate me from my peers. I came to learn later that all that simply meant was that I was called, chosen and entrusted by God to carry the tremendous responsibility of leading His people.

God has a way of separating you from every person on the planet and uniquely calling you as if you were the only one that counts. That is how I felt all through my childhood—that I was separated for some purpose. Of course this caused problems throughout my life, because separation often meant isolation. I really never felt like I fit in most circles and never closely connected with most people that I met or conformed to most rules. I worked hard to overcome that but it only further frustrated me because I was never built to be like that. It was not until I surrendered to the fact that I was uniquely called and my design was His that I found peace with myself and others. I wasn't broken, I was unique.

As believers, we tend to conform to ideas and beliefs of the people around us. What they see as being important; we generally see as important. What they think is right; we tend to accept as being right. We are social creatures who have been subjected to the acceptable views of our society. The church is more social than any other structure usually because the level in which we are accepted will largely depend on our ability to conform. Even in those things that we don't fully agree with, we learn how to conform. We live in a vacuum of others' ideas. Even in places where the scripture is silent, the church creates intent and requires members to conform. This practice alone has alienated people from the church and has separated churches from each other.

We have great battles over what God requires and what was His real intent in scripture. Like the Pharisees, we move from what God said to what we believe He meant, which often places unbearable burdens on the whole body of believers. These mandates have become such an integrated part of the Christian fabric that we have elevated many of these beliefs to the same level as God's Word. But deep inside of us we know that many of the things that we conform to is not what God requires but what those around us require. As believers we have to be able to know the will of God for ourselves. Your life will be filled with many struggles and pitfalls. Unless you have a real knowledge of God's will for you, you will not survive them. If you do not get it for yourself, you will always be subject to the dictates of others.

Thank You for Your Mercy

Jesus meets this woman in Sychar where she was drawing water out of the well. The woman presented to us in St. John chapter 4, was like many people that we see today who tend to think that finding a mate or a companion will be the answer to their lives of loneliness, emptiness, and void. However, what she discovered is that fulfillment can never be achieved through people. In verse 17, He says a very interesting thing to her as He prophesied into her life before the people who had gathered around. *"Thou hast well said I have no husband: for thou hast had five husbands; and he whom thou now hast is not thy husband; in that sadist thou truly"*. He makes the point that the woman has been attempting to satisfy her thirst with things that have no power to fulfill her. How interesting, that after five marriages she continued to seek fulfillment through things that clearly could never fulfill. She thought she could find happiness through the right man. When she didn't find what she needed in the first man; she got rid of him and went to another; and then to another, until she had been married five times. She became frustrated with trying to find "the right man" so she apparently quit marrying and decided to save herself the embarrassment of divorce. She just stayed with him. Her problem wasn't that the men weren't right, but her purpose was flawed. What she didn't understand was she would never be satisfied with people, things, position, or status. The only thing that we will ever acquire in life that has the ability to satisfy us is Christ. Like every person without Christ, she was left with an unquenchable thirst. It was not a physical thirst, because that was her reason for coming to the well in the first place. She knew that the physical water would only satisfy for a season. The real thirst could only be quenched through an active relationship with Jesus.

This story interested me because this woman was Samaritan. Her background was part Jewish and part Babylonian. She would have never been received by the Jews because of her race. But more than that, she was not well received by her own people. She was a woman well known for her sinful reputation and not everyone who looked down on her was lying about her life. The whispers and tales were probably all true, but they failed to see that ostracizing her didn't make them better than her.

She had to be a social outcast who had a reason to be at the well alone. She was loaded down with prejudices, hostilities, and ethnic superiority. She wasn't expecting Jesus to ask her for a drink of water. As a matter of fact, she wasn't expecting Him to say anything to her. She went down to that well with her water pot, no doubt repeating the same routine as she had many times before. However, today was different because she was about to meet the "right man." Jesus asked her for a drink of water. He asked her for what she had when she expected Him to give something to her. It's amazing how Jesus can confront your issues, reveal your shame, and fill your emptiness. Nothing in this world can give everlasting satisfaction like a Word from Jesus.

So often people are convinced that somewhere in the experiences of this world there must be satisfaction! Jesus was making a point to this woman. He was not concerned with her background, how many times she was married, or her religious preference. He was concerned with her brokenness, just as He still is today with our own. God is not concerned with religious rituals. He doesn't really care if we sing contemporary or traditional songs; whether we worship with or without instruments, or which denomination we are affiliated with. He just wants true worship!

I used to wonder if everyone around me saw themselves as being different, unique, or destined like I did. The private conversations that I constantly carry on in my mind always drive me to continue in my pursuits. A voice that refuses to allow me to see things as hopeful and believe that no matter what I've done or what trouble I found myself in, somehow I will get through it. As I grew up, I learned that to some degree all of us carry on those conversations in our mind. Yet, in some people it is often drowned out by the fatigue of their past experiences. I recognize that this same voice is not always God's voice, nor does it always tell the truth about us. I think of the millions of times that I could hear a voice and know that I had something ahead. I wasn't worthy of what was ahead, but I believed that there was something left for me and that would always encourage me.

Often during those times when I met failure, people walked out of my life, lied on me, and even pronounced my ministry dead that I believed that God whispered to me. Through that still small voice He reminded me of who He had called me to be.

Before I go any further, let me just say that I know there are many voices trying to convince us how to live our daily lives. Some of those voices are good; some not so good; and some downright damaging. None of that changes the fact that God is speaking. The voices that we listen to are critical to the life we end up with. We have to examine the number of voices that speak into our lives. Audibly or inaudibly, consciously or unconsciously - we must be able to notice them no matter how well wrapped their disguise.

Aesop, the ancient storyteller, told this fable, "Once upon a time, a donkey found a lion's skin. He tried it on, strutted around, and frightened many animals. Soon a fox came along, and the donkey tried to scare him. But the fox, hearing the donkey's voice, said, If you want to terrify me, you'll have to disguise your bray." Aesop moral: Clothes may disguise a fool, but his words will give him away. When the voices around us attempt to draw us with their hidden motives, no matter how deceptive the cloak, we must recognize those voices as the voices of fools. The scripture tell us in James to try every spirit to see whether they be of God.

We must be ready to allow ourselves to be

interrupted by God. God will constantly send people across our paths, canceling our plans with their claims and petitions. We may pass them and be unmoved because we are preoccupied with more important tasks, or we may ignore the inner workings in our mind to do nothing. We may acknowledge the encounters, examine them and determine what God is saying to us through them. I have chosen to attempt to know God in all my mental impressions, and physical encounters, for fear that I might miss the will of God. I believe that I have always known that my life was filled with purpose. Now, that's not to say that I did not at times live with the concerns of not making it to adulthood or dealing with some tragedy or situation that derailed my purpose. But my union with God reinforced some things that I believed all along. I always believed that my life would make a difference and I refused to die without fulfilling it.

Nevertheless, knowing that doesn't make life easier, neither does it give me carte blanche to live a reckless lifestyle. It is simply a confidence that God will complete what He started in my life regardless of what obstacles come before me. Our lives may take some unexpected turns, but if you believe that you have a purpose, then you have to take whatever happens as being a part of the intentions of God. What I came to understand was I would spend most of my life between endings. Everyday wouldn't be a parade and most of my days would be spent waiting to celebrate instead of in celebration. We know that "in the beginning," the opening of the book of Genesis, God declared things were very good. The end of time will also be very good but we have to make it through the time in between the beginning and the end. God will one day "wipe away every tear" from our eyes. With such a good beginning and ending it may come as a surprise that the middle of our lives will contain sorrows, disappointment, despair, tragedy, and pain. Yet none of it changes the unchanged purpose we have in God. The problem is that we expect uninterrupted good times while in the middle of the story life can take some nasty turns.

What To Do In The Middle

If our lives are to have purpose we need to see that we are living in the middle of a story that was begun and will be concluded by God. My life did not begin with me; it began with God. The search for meaning and healing begins above, and not within. When you read a novel, accidents happen to the characters, but they are not really accidents because the author planned them as part of the story. In life there are no accidents that escape the plan of God. Unless you understand that your success in life lies in your ability to handle the middle, you will in no way succeed.

The Bible records the exodus of the children of Israel as they depart on their relatively short trip across the Sinai Peninsula, but none of them would have imagined the pitfall, battle, struggles, and defeats that they would experience before actually arriving at their destination. Their departure from Egypt is representative of their beginning;

and their arrival in Canaan was the end, but they spent 40 years in the wilderness, which for them was "the middle." Who is really in charge of this world? If not God, then we are left with chaos. If our existence is the result of random and chance origin, then life is without meaning or purpose. Morality would be arbitrary and it wouldn't matter how we lived. Suicidal despair would be a logical conclusion to our meaningless existence. Some people see life as an amazing accident. Even if they are right then what a wonderful accident it is.

God never has to prove Himself to us because He still stands as sovereign apart from us. The first thing we need to understand is that God does not need answers, and He is never surprised by what happens next—we are. Therefore, the focus of our lives must move from God pleasing us, to us pleasing God. That cannot be done unless we are honest about where we are right now in Him. We spend a lot of time trying to convince people around us who we are, when the truth is that we are naked before God and often exposed before each other. It is important that we are open and honest before God. Arthur Pink wrote, "It is Human to err, but it is also human to conceal the blemishes of those we admire." One of the most striking discoveries about scripture is that the Word of God reveals the errors of even its greatest heroes. For example, the Bible talks specifically about Noah's failure: He is called a man of the soil and a farmer; but also a reminder of the Adamic comparison, "just another human." He was a drunk who laid uncovered. The way in which he fell asleep was not an accident, but a consequence of the sin of drunkenness. Anyone who has been drunk understands that drunkenness loosens one's inhibitions and causes one to do things when he otherwise would be ashamed. We all have shortcomings and consequences to bear as a result of our choices. God already knows what you've done. So, be honest and tell Him all about it. He wants to extend His forgiveness and mercy to you.

Keep Hope Alive 4

However, all of us regardless of how damaged we are or how difficult our condition remain hopeful that our change is still coming. For many believers our reality is often disfigured, but our hope remains intact, that brighter days are ahead. The dreams of what we desire to become will be realized in this present world. The Psalmist records in Psalm 27:13, "I had fainted, unless I had believed to see the goodness of the Lord in the land of the living." I think I understand David better, that no matter how difficult life becomes and how terminal the straits that I may find myself facing; I will rise with a hopeful heart because of my belief that the goodness of God will be demonstrated while I am still alive. I remain hopeful that somehow God will deliver me, or vindicate me when it's gone beyond my hope. I am eternally hopeful because of Christ. My hope in Christ allows me to be damaged and yet still dream about a future that defies my present situations or circumstances.

Saved By Grace and Works

There were times where I would ask myself the question, "Am I free?" That seems silly today, but for believers who are trying to please God it's not that silly. We are told that we live now by the liberty of Christ, but are often confused when it comes to those times when we have the occasional mishap or event that we know does not please Christ. Romans 6:16-19 says, *"Don't you know that when you offer yourselves to someone as obedient slaves, you are slaves of the one you obey –whether you are slaves to sin, which leads to death, or to obedience, which leads to righteousness."* This makes it clear, that when I surrender to sin that I freely offer myself as a slave to the devil.

So my first battle is the tension that exists in knowing who I am, because there is often a war happening in me about me. Other people's assessment of me was hurtful, but I believe it was hurtful because I had not come to understand who I was. I was often guilty of what they said and found myself serving the sin instead of serving righteousness when I knew that it would please God.

The wages of sin and the gifts of God have always been on display among Christians. Questions such as, "How far can you go and still be a recipient of the saving grace of God in your life; How many and what kind of works are needed to be pleasing in the sight of God; and to what degree or at what combination do we need to reach in order to be considered ready to go to heaven?" This is the issue of Law verses Grace. John 1:17 says, *"The law came by Moses, but grace and truth came through Jesus."* Though I have an argument with those who totally detach from the constraints of the law; I cannot ignore the clear revelation of Jesus' work found in the scripture.

I'm going to do my best to be more biblical than denominational when talking about my freedom in Christ. Before you feel the need to rip this page out of this book, hear me out when it comes to my liberty in Christ Jesus. The tension between our liberty in Christ and our responsibility to Him is not newly developed in the church, and it's not denominationally segregated or ethnically identifiable. We cannot, through systematic theology bring a case to one side that would overwhelm the proponents of the other side. We can however, see it clearly in the old covenant Bible, where the prominent position would be law.

Before the covenant was handed to Moses by God there was a sense of wanting to know how to please God, going all the way back to Adam and his descendant Abraham. Abraham is the father of not only the Jewish people who were the recipients of the law of God, but all of the three great monotheistic faith's trace their origins back to Abraham, which are Judaism, Christianity, and Islam. This is important because in order to follow the rule of God it is necessary to agree on who God is and then what rule will we use as being the authentic word of God. Of course, there is much disagreement about faith documents among these three religions but all will agree that there is only one God.

If we framed the debate today, it would fall under the heading of Law and Grace. No one would question the fact that the Law is the word of God and the authentic document handed to Moses on Mt. Sinai as a guide map to His will for His chosen people of Israel. There are many scholars and religious groups who feel that without any word abdicating the law and its requirements, we as Christians are required to apply those laws that we find in the Old and New Testament teachings which are that good works of benevolence, honesty, righteous living, and soberness will save men. Then there are those who believe that the Old Testament is past and should have no impact on the New Testament believers. Finally, there are those who believe that there is some combination that should be sought. The relationship of Law and Grace is critical for us to understand today and it was something I struggled to understand for years. Instead of living in the liberty of Christ, I would keep count of the times I failed to meet the standards that I felt was necessary for me to please Christ. First, let me tell those of you who are still keeping count that even in your best days you will fail to keep the law and no measure of weight system is going to work for you because if you fail to keep one of the laws, then you are guilty of breaking them all. I thank God continually that He kept the law absolutely so I wouldn't have to.

The good works and righteous living I do before God has not earned me the favor of God. In fact, after all we have been given by God, right living is only reasonable to be expected by Him. Paul clearly states in Romans 6:14,"..for ye are not under the law, but under grace." The Law was never given to believers as a way to give us a standard by which to live, but it was given to show us how far from the standard does all men live. Paul makes the greatest case to the Galatians about freedom from the Law; In Galatians 3:1-3, *"Foolish Galatians, who hath bewitched you, that ye should not obey the truth, before whose eyes Jesus Christ hath been evidently set forth, crucified among you? This only would I learn of you, Received ye the Spirit by the works of the law, or by the hearing of faith? Are you so foolish? Having begun in the Spirit, are ye now made perfect by the flesh?"* We didn't come to be in Christ or more in Christ by keeping the law, in fact you become more of a sinner by attempting to keep the Law. Remember Ephesians 2:8, where it says, "We are saved by grace through faith..." Look at this, Galatians 3:23-25 *"But before faith came, we were kept under the law, shut up unto the faith which should afterwards be revealed. Wherefore the law was our schoolmaster to bring us unto Christ, that we might be justified by faith. But after that faith is come, we are no longer under a schoolmaster."* Did you see it, we are "no longer under a schoolmaster", and we are no longer under it because we no longer need it. No longer is there a need for a measuring stick, or proof to show that we have drifted from God, because through the work of Jesus, we have all been reconciled back to God. Some are more Calvinistic and reformed in your thinking about grace and I agree that it does sound too easy. However, I am not the one who made it easy. Jesus made it easy by offering Himself as a sacrifice and since He became the acceptable sacrifice, I find it foolish to keep trying to be one.

This is the good news "gospel." Jesus, for all of us, became that "new and living way which He consecrated for us, through His own flesh." Out of gratitude I freely give myself over as an unworthy sacrifice, but it's not because I believe it will make me more holy, but because it is my reasonable service. Since the work has been completely done by Him, I no longer lose my faith when I find those areas that are not perfected in me. We are under grace and not the law. Legalism verse Grace, and anyone who studied the Puritans and the establishment of the Massachusetts Bay Colony in the 15th century understand that these Puritans were a collection of godly men and women who arrived in North America seeking liberty from the increasing corrupt Church of England. They had dreams of conducting a holy experiment of providing a colony of people who could serve God without corruption, but with love and unity. The problem here is most people who read this book, without little dissention would agree that the puritans were legalist. But in their day they would have been considered not only legalist, but also reformist.

Our understanding of legalism today is generally born out of the example of the Pharisees in the time of Jesus. They were constantly in conflict with Jesus not because of their commitment to the law, but because of their failure to understand the spirit of the law. Again, had you lived during the period of Hellenization and knew the origin of the Pharisees you would have called them reformist. There intent was not to misapplying the law, but men who wanted to ensure that the people did not depart from the law. Many use the definition of legalism as a form of works as a way to salvation and righteousness. The problem here is that some biblical scholars point out that we are not saved by what we do, but based on what God did for us by offering Jesus. Ephesians 2:8 says, *"For by grace are ye saved through faith; and that not of yourselves, it is the gift of God."* This doesn't mean that we have a license to fail to do the will of God in our lives or sin without regard. In Galatians 5:13-15 we are told, *"For, brethren, ye have been called unto liberty; only use not liberty for an occasion to the flesh, but by love serve one another."* These truths have been difficult for some because to them, this suggests that it is not necessary to live according to God's command at all and one can still gain eternal life.

The first key is to be sure that all scripture is understood in its context and to avoid the isogetically liberties that are often attempted by those who are trying to find their point in a text. I don't believe grace causes sin to increase when properly taught. To the contrary, once you come to a full understanding of grace, you should be motivated to please Him. No one believes that salvation by grace means there is no consequences for sin. There is more to be gained in life here and the life to come than heaven. There is favor and rewards in the life to come that is awaiting all of us who are faithful until death. But no amount of faithfulness can result in an individual being saved. Good works have its privileges but heaven isn't one of them. How is it that the more I learned about God, and longed to pleased Him that I seemed to consistently fail in my life to conform to the commands of God? I was damaged.

Now all these years later, sadly I confess that I'm still damaged. Yes, I said that I am still damaged. I must be because the perfection that has been commanded of me remains elusive despite every effort, strategy, and spiritual solution offered by the most revered in this present day faith. I have read, attended conferences, consumed myself in activities designed to distract and equip me, prayed long prayers for long periods of time to heal me: But with all of that, I must still be damaged because there is still sin found in me. Perhaps I'm better at detecting it, and maybe I am more aware of it, because I will admit that there are victories and deliverances in areas of my life. A crazy thing has happened, I can think of some areas where I had overcome in my past but I'm still fighting them again now.

Gone But Not Forgotten   5

I know I've done a great deal of discussion about the systemic problems in expecting perfections from imperfect flesh. I want to be careful to make sure that we lay the blame properly at the feet of the one who is to blame. With all the interferences in life and the demons that have been assigned to destroy your life, and believe me there are devils assigned to destroy your future; the only serious threat to you is you. The biggest enemy of me is in me. In Romans 6:18-20, we read the most condemning section of text for anyone who seeks to blame others for their failure to meet the dictates of Christ in their flesh. *"Being then made free from sin, you became the servants of righteousness. I speak after the manner of men because of the infirmity of your flesh: for as you have yielded your members as servants to uncleanness and to iniquity; even so now yield your members servants to righteousness to holiness. For when you were servants of sin, you were free from righteousness."*

The key is the slavery experienced by me and by you is by choice and slavery comes in many different flavors. The enslavement of carnal pleasure, "If it feels good....do it."

This is prominent because this slavery will cause a person to disregard the consequences to themselves or to others. Few people will argue that many people have become enslaved by popularity and acclaim. Peer pressure in the church is a very real elixir. The pressure of desiring acceptance, confirmation, and sometimes advancement in the church has led many to compromise their real beliefs. This is a direct result of the spirit of this world, called the *pride of life*. What is really sad is most people seeking the approval of others, do so without regard to gaining the approval of God. Paul said an interesting thing in Galatians 1:10, *"For am I now seeking the approval of man, or of God? Or am I trying to please man? If I were still trying to please man, I would not be a servant of Christ."* This is enormously relevant to this discussion but is also the reason why so many people have not gained the liberty of Christ in their lives. For many people, their value is connected to the things they possess. What they have is the only way they can judge who they are, and they use this measurement to perceive how other people judge them. They see all of their human value in what they earn, where they work and where they may live. Words like integrity, sacrifice, and character are subservient to the desire to get wealth. In 1 Timothy 5:10 Paul wrote to his young protégé Timothy and said, *"For the love of money is the root of all kinds of evil, for which some have strayed from the faith in their greediness, and pierced themselves through with many sorrows."* It is amazing how money has dominated our society and nearly everyone in it. "Cold cash" is the goal for too many people because our society has made gaining more money a reflection of your importance and the church has followed suit. Now the preachers and the rappers are saying essentially the same thing, "Get rich or die trying."

The question I would ask here is "What if people knew you?" Not the sanitized version of you that took you this long to develop. I'm talking about your secrets, your thoughts, and those incidents that you already decided to forget and never confess. This too is part of what you are and it would seem to me that really accepting me would in some ways include the ugly possibilities of me. Make no bones about it; all of us are living with some ugly possibilities. In Romans 7:18, Paul was so transparent when he said, *"For I know that nothing good dwells in me, that is, in my flesh. For I have desired to do what is right, but not the ability to carry it out."* I had to conclude this sentiment about myself that in spite of all the great sermons that were delivered and the people who I work so hard not to disappoint, when stripped to the truth of who I am, I was left with the phrase from Paul, "that nothing good dwells in me." It is a liberating admission and an empowering revelation to know that with all of my efforts to please God and people I had long concluded that my efforts were focused on pleasing myself. I discovered that there had to be something more and pleasing God had little to do with how I am perceived by people.

While everyone is fighting over positions and talking about their possessions, the church does not seem to realize that these are indications that we are not pleasing God, but pleasing our flesh. It is the old self that we are submitting to and still trying to please. We are told in Romans 6:6 that *"Knowing this, that our old man is crucified with him, that the body of sin might be destroyed, that henceforth we should not serve sin."* God is not as concerned with us having a fine house and big car as we are. The real promises of God has very little to do with attaining things on this earth. The real promises are for future spiritual homes, peace, forgiveness of sin, and eternal life; Not cars, not position, or money. People have a tendency to be impressed by you based on things that have nothing to do with the promises of God.

Many believers often find themselves living under the influence of that part of them that is supposed to be gone. The scripture refers to him as the "old man." Ephesians 4:22 says, *"That ye put off concerning the former conversation of the old man, which is corrupt according to the deceitful lusts.."* This old man includes this mortal body with all of its proclivities and commands. At first this seems to present a contradiction in these two scriptures, because in Romans we are told that the "old man" is dead, but in Ephesians, we are told to put him away, which seems to suggest that he doesn't fall off, but we must put him off. Generally, we are told that the "old man" is our sinful nature, but this is where I have difficulty because the scripture is not telling us that we have some nature in us that died. They say that we died; consider the following offerings: Romans 6:2 says, *"God forbid. How shall we, that are dead to sin, live any longer therein?"* Romans 6:7 states, *"For he that is dead is freed from sin."* We are dead to sin. According to verse four we were baptized into His death. *"We were buried with him by baptism into death; we have been planted together in the likeness of his death; we shall be also in the likeness of his resurrection."* (Romans 6:4-6). So you died: The person you were before you were saved, that person died.

The good news is that you are now alive again according to 2 Corinthians 5:17. Now in order to really get this, we have to depart from the literal sense and understand that He is really using this as a figure of speech. Being dead to sin doesn't mean that I'm dead to the nature of sin. This is the problem that some people have because they have concluded that if they still lust in their flesh, then they are not saved enough. It's not the nature that has died; rather it is the relationship with sin that has died. Look at Romans 7:6, *"But now we are delivered from the law, that being dead wherein we were held; that we should serve in newness of spirit, and not in the oldness of the letter."* This is clearer because it causes us to know that what happened to us through Christ. We ended the relationship with the law and we are now under a new relationship with grace. Final point, Paul wrote to the Colossians in chapter 3:9, *"Lie not one to another, seeing that ye have put off the old man with his deeds (10) And have put on the new man, which is renewed in knowledge after the image of him that created him."* This was an admonition to change their behavior and that's the challenge for us.

There is no magic bullet to keep us from unrighteous acts except staying away from unrighteous acts. Galatians 5:24 says, *"And they that are Christ's have crucified the flesh with the affections and lusts."* This sounds like a responsibility for us, not something that has been taken away from us. Paul said, "I die daily," and that's all the proof I need to know that sin nature didn't die, because there will be no need for Paul to kill it and then no need for him to kill it on a daily basis.

These are the realities that harmed my relationship with God and with some people. I've discovered that I have to decide that I'm going to overcome my desire and walk in obedience to the will of God. It is easy to live in denial and keep searching for some place where you are no longer tempted. This generally resulted in you disappointing yourself and disappointing others. In fact, I wanted to please everyone to the degree that I became legalistic and wanted to be celebrated for living according to God's command, which was really only what I was supposed to do. Contrastly, I wanted to ignore and justify the many times I failed to be all that He called me to be. However, I failed to address the real issues in my life, which was the problem of not being totally surrendered to God. I would preach all my best "get off my back sermons." One of my favorites was Romans 3:23, "All have sinned and fallen short of the glory of God," while I pretty much stayed away from such as Romans 6:23 that said, *the wages of sin is death, but the gift of God is eternal life in Christ Jesus our Lord"* Or John 3:3 which says, *"Verily, verily, I say unto you, except a man is born again, he cannot see the kingdom of God."* All because I failed to understand that my "old man" was still with me, but it was my job to be sure that he didn't enter again in relationship with me.

What has to be understood from all this is that life has

an eternal purpose and must be lived from an eternal perspective. Before any of us can demonstrate the ability to overcome the issue of sin, we must first show the ability to overcome our will. This requires a transformation of the heart, a renovation of our character and a complete alteration of our attitude. We should understand that without Jesus a change of character is almost meaningless, and an adjustment of attitudes is insufficient. There comes a time in our life when we need to check our self to see what needs correcting or changed. Our life should always be in a state of development. Never become complacent where you feel you don't need any improvement or enhancements in your life. Whether it is a spiritual, financial, or physical, there is always room for greater change. Why? Because the bible said in Romans 8:7, that the carnal mind is enmity against God. There is a side of me that is resisting having a mind like His. I can be stubborn. I oftentimes have to consider what I say because too often what comes out of me does not represent Christ well. Our conversation easily reveals who is in control of us at the time.

Jesus looked at His most developed disciple and instead of rebuking him; Jesus rebuked the mind that had control of him. He told Peter, *"Get thee behind me, for thou savourest not the things that be of God, but the things that be of men."* In other words, you are talking crazy. You are so connected to the world, that when you speak, you show that everything that is important to you is in this world.

When you speak, what do you say, God stuff or world stuff? I'm in a fight because I really want to prove that

I'm relevant but my relevancy is steeped in carnality. How I am supposed to feel will make no sense to those who don't know how Jesus thought. Forgiving when I have been wronged and repairing what has been broken seems to be crazy when it never was your fault. But the part of you that is just like Him will say I forgive you because I don't have the right to hold this thing against you. It's in my mind and if I want to be free my thinking has to move out of the way and give way to His thinking. Every thought must be brought under subjection to the obedience of Christ. I'm making my mind obey. Even in those times when I want to obey but retaliate, I surrender my *right* so that I can become what He wants. I want to know Him in the power of His resurrection and in the fellowship of His suffering. Right now I'm joined to His suffering because I know that there is a reward. I start talking to my mind and command it not to be negative, discouraged, sick or angry.

As a man thinks in his heart so is he; there comes a time when I have to audit my surroundings, my company, and some people. The reason for doing an audit, is so that you will have clear picture of past performances and will be able to make some decisions about what you are able to do going forward. There may be some people that you can't handle now because your audit showed that there was a negative impact in your past. You may have to be careful with some people because you had them in the wrong column. You may have had them listed as an asset but you then discovered that they were a liability. You may not necessarily get rid of them, but reassessment of your relationship needs to take place. There are some people I don't have in my circle because I can't afford them. I can't afford what they are putting in my mind, bringing to my life or what they are putting in my ear. I simply can't afford it. If I don't have control over myself at the time, I don't need to be around anyone who cares nothing about the spirit.

Whenever I am in places like Chicago I like to work on my mall ministry. Once, I was there and I knew I didn't need to spend money because I was already counting the cost and knew that I had other things that had to be done. But my mind was saying, "You only live once; you work hard and you ain't leaving nothing to your children or I'll figure it out when I get home." I begin to say to myself, "I need to stop acting like a baby because I'm a grown man and the devil ain't going to talk me out of my responsibility." I began to rebuke that mind. The only reason I'm having a problem with my flesh is because of what my mind is telling my flesh. If my mind gives my flesh the wrong signals, my flesh will not end up doing the right thing. If I tell my mind to give God praise, it will praise Him.

Romans 7:15 says, *"For what I would do, that do I not, and the thing that I should allow I ended up denying permission. But that I hate, that I do."* I hate that I can't stop drinking but I'm drinking; I hate that I can't stop lying, but I'm really just a liar; I hate that I'm cheating but I'm still cheating. I want to get a raise but I don't want to go to work; I want to be loved but everybody that loves me I seem to put them through it; I want to be happy but I do stuff that is sad. Romans 8:9 tells us, *"But you are no longer (in control) of the flesh, but of the spirit if so be that the Spirit of God dwell in you. And if any man has not the Holy Ghost, he is none of His."*

I don't care how saved and anointed you are, nothing can happen unless you allow it. God has the power to change and fix you. How you think will determine what you have and what you can do. Nothing can move without faith. The word of God is so powerful that you don't have to hear it. You can read it and be set free. You don't have to even be in the room, because the word can be declared for your freedom in one place and someone can receive the manifestation of that word 2000 miles away because of the anointing of the Holy Ghost. Romans 7:17 says, *"Now then it is no more I that do it, but sin that dwelleth in me."* Now wait because this can be confusing, because I just said that the Holy Ghost dwells in me. There must be some confusion because I also have sin dwelling in the same place in me. Now that's a fight, because whenever you have two things talking to you, you have to determine who you are going to listen to. There are times when what sin wants me to do drowns out what God is commanding me to do.

And Isaac entreated the Lord for his wife, because she was barren: and the Lord was entreated of him, and Rebekah his wife conceived. And the children struggled together within her (Genesis 25:21). Isaac being a type of Christ prays that God would send a blessing, but before the blessing comes, he sends struggle. Two nations are in you and they will struggle. There is a blessing in you, but in order for it to produce there will be trouble. They are a blessing but in order to see them as a blessing, you will have to survive the struggle. Now I know you want to be blessed in every season but there are two things warring inside of you and there is going to be a struggle inside of you. A part of you and me resists the mind of God. You might think that it was never supposed to be like this and you were never supposed to be discouraged. You must understand that there is a war that is happening while you are worshipping. The spiritual and carnal mind is warring against one another. Part of you that desires to do the will of God, and a part that does not care one bit about it, even though they are dwelling in the same house. Paul said that these two parts focus in opposite directions and they are constantly in conflict. *"For the flesh lusteth against the Spirit, and the Spirit against the flesh: and they are contrary the one to the other"* (Galatian 5:17).

When it comes to the "old nature," we may starve it to the point that it has no strength to manifest through fasting. Anybody who has been on a fast will tell you that it is like dieting and losing weight. It has the desired effect of losing the weight but the moment you go back to eating, you will find yourself putting back on more than you took off. The same is true with the "old man." We are fine as long as we starve it, but don't make the mistake of releasing it, because it will desire more than it did before. The only way to control the habits and appetites of the "old man" is to continually walk in the "new man" by feeding it the right spiritual food. That's the part that you wish were gone, but as long as you are alive, the fight will continue because he's not going anywhere.

Broken System

One of the biggest hindrances to faith in God (and you might want to hold on to your seatbelts) is the insistence of every denomination in America to be privy to some special revelation of knowledge. I believe that there is such a thing as absolute truth but I don't believe it is shrouded in secrecy and confusion. How is it that everyone has a greater revelation and a larger more perfected truth than that is already given? Why is it necessary to show ones' uniqueness by pointing out some obscure portion of scripture that no one else has ever considered? Much like in Acts 17:18-20 where it says, *"There were certain philosophers of the Epicureans, and of the Stoics, encountered him. And some said, "What will this babbler say?" Some, He seemeth to be a setter forth of strange gods: because he preached unto them JESUS, and the resurrection. And they took him, and brought him unto Areopagus, saying, May we know what this new doctrine, whereof thou speakest, is? For thou bringest certain strange things to our ears: we would know therefore what these things mean."* There seems to be this unexplainable thirst for some new thing to the point today that it outweighs their search for truth. Churches are widely divided over the issue of what is pleasing to God and the lack of resolution among religious authorities and organizations about what is pleasing to God leaves great latitude about what is permitted and what is not permitted for Christians.

What should a believer do in order to know that He is in the will of God? How does he or she deal with certain issues like salvation, repentance or deliverance? There are people who are frustrated church members who are doing all they can to please God, but the separate beliefs in them make it difficult for Christians to know what is really required. For example, some denominations think it's okay to drink and others strictly forbid any alcohol in their body. What impact do these different messages have on the Christian who desires to please God? What about the guilt of being told that you are out of the will of God or what you may have done is a sin. Then there is the peer guilt of failing to live up to certain requirements. How much weight should be placed on these requirements and those found in scripture? Does the number of denominational differences help or hurt believers seeking God? How does a person know what really is sin and what is the real remedy for sin? Does it cause some believers to give up and live outside of structure as a result of this doctrinal disunity?

I believe the real brokenness is not as much in the individual as it is in the systemic corruption that can sometimes be found in the church. What is required by God and required by the church is rarely the same. Perhaps because it's difficult to segregate the cultural, political, and personal mandates from the spiritual ones. In other words, when within yourself, you don't believe it is healthy to drink alcohol, it is difficult not to apply those beliefs to everyone else, whether God requires it or not. The true message of Christ can be often overshadowed by an eager and zealous servant who simply wants to avoid getting too close to the line. The result may end up being that they find themselves moving the line further and further to their own self-righteous ends than God's ends. Consequently, the people who desire to live within the dictates of God's word are often defeated because of the raised stakes and blurred lines of self-righteousness. God has a standard of good and evil and we often see that standard presented in scripture. We see God issuing directives and commands for people to live by; to not commit murder (Genesis 9:5-6) which was the law given to Israel (Exodus 20).

I don't want to do anything to diminish the personal responsibility for each of us because I believe as a whole we spend too much of our time deflecting and casting blame on others when others are never the problem. Sometimes, we are just simply out of the will of God.

I Didn't Deserve That

Life has a subtle way of bringing retroprocity to your life that you never thought was coming. When things happen they rarely seem fair. I mean, everybody can look back and attach some behaviors or actions to their current troubles, but even so, that is no way to really tell why your present condition exists. Sometimes it feels like the punishment doesn't always match the crime. We just have agreed that life happens; or is there something more intentional about everything that happens in our lives?

We know from the scriptures that we have been predestined. *"For (those) whom He foreknew, He also predestined to be conformed to the image of His Son, that He might be the firstborn among many brethren. Moreover, (those) whom He predestined these He also called, whom He called these He also justified; and whom He justified, these He also glorified"* (Romans 8:29-30). In other words, this is an act of God from eternity before time began, by which God not only foreknew, but actually because of what He already knew, He chose you for certain things to produce glory for Himself through your life. It had to happen. In order to benefit the kingdom there were some things that had to be changed in you. I am convinced that the things that happen to you are used to either correct you; to change you, or to get glory out of you. It is going to take God to make something out of us that He can use. When everyone else said that I couldn't make it or that I was past my season, I found out that God still can and did. I have learned not to be mad at anyone for not agreeing or approving of my journey, because it was God who authored my journey. I must praise Him for not putting more on me than I am able to bear.

Let's just shut some things down; the people that hated you shouldn't mean anything to you because what you need they can't provide and if they had it, many of them still wouldn't provide it. I like knowing that whatever they do to you can't stop God from blessing you. Don't let anyone stress you out. God knew who to send to oppose you. Their opposition is used to prepare you for what He is attempting to produce in you. Other people's opinions or their opposition will never have anything to do with the blessings that are about to overtake you. They only have power over you because you still don't believe God's journey for you. But God can't release anything to you until He knows that He can trust you, even though He called you. God calls Jonah to go preach to Nineveh, but instead of focusing on the assignment that God had for him, he was more concerned with what the Ninevites did to him. So God had to swallow him up. It would have been easy for him to proclaim that he was in the belly of the fish because of the Ninevites. But Jonah was there because of himself. I had to realize that in my own life. It wasn't about other people, it was about me. The Ninevites were a problem of his past, but he is the one who invited them into his present and was ready to take them into his future. Okay, let me talk about myself because I have had those times when I think I'm right in holding people to what they did against me. Isn't that a trip? Because when we are in the right we want restitutions. We make people pay for messing up, hurting and mistreating us. We can be awfully bitter for years over something that we can hardly remember the details of. How is it that you can want so much to happen to others when they have wronged us, but won't even apologize when you've backstabbed someone else? Some things may be chaotic in our lives because of our unwillingness to move on and forgive people who have offended us. Some things you must let go. The real problem is not what they did. I had to realize that myself. Some things were not a result of their actions and how I was mistreated, but it was all about my out of control ego that told me that I did not deserve to be wronged. I realized that I was acting humble but all the time hoping that God would curse them. I was full of revenge and looking for ways to sabotage others and get them back. I'm not by myself, because your real problem is not people, you haven't figure out that the godly will have to suffer too; the only way that God is going to know that He can trust you is to test you. This means that you will be hurt, let down and held up. You may have prayers that seem that they will not be answered and go through barren and dry seasons. Until you can be told "No" by God and your love for Him remain the same you are not mature.

I had to come to the understanding that I may be preaching, but I needed to grow up and be willing to suffer. I had to stop telling God what I wanted and learn how to be alright with what He wants for me. Don't waste your life being dominated by what happened because God knows how to use what happened. You may be mad because you were hurt, but God allowed that heartache because He wanted to bring to your attention that there is something in you that needs to die - like your opinion. Some of us have the nerve to magnify other people's wrong doing and miss seeing our own. You need to relax and believe that vengeance is the Lord's and that He knows how to deliver the godly. He will prepare a table before you in the presence of your enemy. All you have to do is hurry up and figure out that that issues are in the past, and release people so that you can move forward with your life. You have pouted long enough; you've been self-righteous long enough; you've had a pity party for yourself long enough. It's time to start running again.

Pharaoh, I Thought You Said I Can Leave

"Stand fast therefore in the liberty wherewith Chris hath made us free, and be not entangled again with the yoke of bondage" Galatians 5:1. I am interested in the biblical terminology of deliverance from sin and if you are delivered from sin; what does that mean? Does it mean that we no longer sin; are we delivered from specific sins or are we referring to the number of sins? What are the circumstances that will draw us back to sin? What are the consequences of sin? Why do Christians struggle so much with sin? What about Moses and Pharaoh and the circumstances that led Pharaoh to release the children of Israel, but then turn and chase them again; why is it that sin seems to be chasing us? The problem with Israel was their language; it was the language of surrender. When you talk the language of surrender it's not a long step from actually surrendering. In their case you would have thought that God had proven that after 10 plagues that He was absolutely sovereign over Pharaoh. However, they were still behaving like God had not showed them that He is over the elements and over all people and every obstacle.

What are we going to do? That is the question we ask sometimes when we are facing challenges and temptations in our life. We act like we do not know what to do when all there is to do is trust God. Stand still and see the salvation of the Lord and not your own.

I remember purchasing a tape recorder once (for those who remember what that is) from a department store.

When I got it home, I can remember being very excited because I had imagined all the ways I would be able to listen to the music I liked and the freedom it afforded. I recall opening the box and reading the instructions carefully to ensure that I would get maximum use and full potential of the recorder; sounds, special effects, etc. After reading all the instructions and trying all of the knobs, I could never get the recorder to do all that the instructions said it would do. I eventually took it back to the store and asked them why it wasn't working the way the manufacturer stated. After some examination of the product, they discovered that it was damaged and replaced it with another recorder.

This was what I used to think about myself. I thought, "I must be damaged." These feelings were driven by my experience within the church. When I came into the church I was told that since I had been chosen to live for Christ, that if I would work hard enough I should never know weakness, sorrow, lust, anger, or bitterness. So I was left with two possible conclusions; that I must be damaged, or this lifestyle that I'm striving for is impossible to gain. I made these conclusions because I honestly felt as if I had made my best efforts at perfection and failed. As I began to make an honest assessment of each day, I was always left feeling that I blew it again. I felt like Paul in Romans 7:21 when he said, "I find then a law, that, when I would do good, evil is present with me." After making my best effort to submit, focus on God, and bring under subjection the appetites of the flesh, I still didn't find that I was without guilt. As a result, instead of perfecting broken places in my life, I became self-righteous about the things that I did not do. I began to think that because I did not do certain things or have certain problems that I must be better than those who did them.

From the moment I declared salvation in Jesus, I sincerely tried to be true and committed in my relationship with God. However, I don't want to suggest that my efforts to resist the desires of my flesh weren't greatly impacted by my increased focused. In fact, as I studied the word of God and continued with the fellowship of believers, I found that it did become easier to resist some areas of sin. Consequently, I felt in those areas that I became a vessel more pleasing to God. But most of the time, I was tormented by my seeming inability to meet the expectations that were placed on me by myself and others. Everything I did, everyone I met, every thought I had became a threat to my relationship with God. I felt like I was being dishonest even when I knew that my intentions were sincere.

One of the greatest books I ever read is *The Practice of the Presence of God: The Best Rule of A Holy Life,* by an Augustinian Monk named Nicholas Hermanc (known as Brother Lawrence) who lived in the 17th Century. This book is a timeless spiritual classic of a young believer who had a spiritual awakening to the presence of God in the world and began to understand the divine presence in the simplest of tasks in life. While he served in the monastery and did menial tasks like cooking and cleaning, he saw the honor and duty to serve God and to discipline his heart to always be aware of the presence of God. There is nothing more awe striking than to practice being aware of God's presence in everything you do. I read this book often. Especially in those times when I become aware that Brother Lawrence's practice should also be my practice, that I am really nothing in the presence of God. One of the things that he said was, "I regard myself as the most wretched of all men, stinking and covered with sores, and as one who has committed all sorts of crimes against his King. Overcome by remorse; I confess all my wickedness to Him, ask His pardon and abandon myself entirely to Him to do with as He will. But this King filled with goodness and mercy, far from chastising me, lovingly embraces me, makes me eat at His table, serves me with His own hands, gives me the keys of His treasures and treats me as His favorite. He talks with me and is delighted with me in a thousand and one ways. He forgives me and relieves me of my principle bad habits without talking about them. I beg Him to make me according to His heart and always the more weak and despicable I see myself to be, the more beloved I am of God." This is really how my life has been before God. I have disappointed him yet he has returned it by loving me.

I would often wonder out loud if anyone in the church was meeting the restrictions that I was asking of myself. I've been involved in church nearly all my life and have heard some disturbing stories of men and women "falling" to the temptations of their flesh; shunned because of some visible failure in their lives. I've seen people who were faithful succumb to some area of weakness and as a result they were disdained. I've seen lives broken, powerful people brought to their knees, and God-loving people return to a life where God was not present.

In Max Lucado's book, *He Still Moves Stones,* he writes of the incident we find in John 8, using an illustration: He tells of a woman name Rebecca Thompson who fell twice from Fremont Canyon Bridge and suggested that she died both times. The first fall broke her heart; the second broke her neck. I know he is using some license but the point is clear. In his illustration she was only eighteen years of age when she and her 11 year old sister were abducted by a couple of men in Wyoming. They drove the girls forty miles to the Fremont Canyon Bridge. Then they brutally beat them and raped Rebecca. She somehow convinced them not to do the same to her sister Amy. Both were thrown over the bridge into a narrow gorge. Amy died when she landed on a rock near the river but Rebecca slammed into a ledge and was ricocheted into deeper water. With a hip fractured in five places, she struggled to shore. She was eventually found and the physicians treated her wounds, and the courts imprisoned her attackers. Nineteen years later, she returned to the bridge and drove 70 mph into the North Platte River: And that's when Rebecca Thompson died her second death. The truth of this story was despite Rebecca's attractive smile and appealing personality, friends say that she struggled with the ugly fact that she survived but her little sister did not. Everyone she knew and thousands that she didn't know had heard the humiliating details of her tragedy. She had been raped, violated, and shamed. It is always difficult for me to retell this story without feeling helpless and sorrowful for Rebecca and Amy's tragedy.

What is worse is that the church is full of people who have tragedies that are rarely told, and incidents impact their lives in ways that cause them to self-destruct. The greater tragedy is that in the same way that people only saw Rebecca and the humiliating details of her rape and shame. Week after week the church is full of people who instead of being celebrated for surviving, are criticized because of what has happened in their life. Sometimes we live with our canyons of shame from situations we never asked for and things we never intended to do. Sometimes our shame is public. Whether you are branded by a divorce you did not want; contaminated by a disease you never expected or marked by a handicap you didn't create. Whether it is in your imagination or in the reality of others, you have been marked. You may have been labeled a divorcee, an invalid, an orphan, or an AIDS patient. You may have been pushed to the edge by an abusive spouse, molested by a perverted parent, living with a spirit of anger, jealousy, or lust. No one else knows; but you know and that's enough. Unless you get help, the dawn will never come.

You should not be surprised when I say that there are Rebecca Thompson's in every city and Fremont Bridges in every town. There are many Rebecca Thompson's in the Bible. But the woman in John 8 embodies them all. We don't get to peep into her life enough to understand what it was about her that led her to adultery and the Bible doesn't even try and justify the act or defend her innocence. In fact, the text tells us that she was caught in the very act. The only thing I see that was done right in this story is that the Pharisees brought the woman to Jesus. I will leave it to you, as the reader, to go to the scriptures for the details of this story. But what I need to point out from the text is Jesus' words to the crowd that had gathered together for the woman's stoning. *"Anyone here who has never sinned cast the first stone."* Talk about being, a party-crasher, and a breath-taker. To have Jesus look at the requirements of the law and say to them "Okay, let's get started, but who is worthy to throw the first rock?" This became a revelation to me. It liberated me to no longer be paralyzed by my failures as I worked toward the perfection of God. In this parable, no one was found worthy to throw the first rock. It's not fair for you to deflect attention from your errors while putting a spotlight onto mine. Romans 2:1 tells us, *"Therefore thou art inexcusable, O man, whosoever thou art that judges: for therein thou judgest another, thou condemnest thyself; for thou that judgest doest the same things."* I would like to ask this question. What are you going to do with your stones? Be careful that you don't use a judgmental attitude against others to cover the problems in your own heart.

If we would spend less time trying to convince others that we are god-like and prepare ourselves to be god-like, we would be more tolerable of other people's situations. Let's be honest, all of us are unworthy, broken, and damaged. I don't pretend to know what happened to you that left you broken, nor do I know exactly how I got damaged. I've spent the last two decades of my life trying to avoid showing my areas of weakness and admitting my nakedness when all this time I found out that I wasn't hidden—that was a true word from Heaven for me. Just knowing this caused me to move forward and forget about the shame and guilt. I had to come to understand that God loved me because He knew about everything that was unresolved and unfixed in me. He knew that I was bringing all of my issues with me into this faith. I came to understand that there were things in my life that I struggled to overcome that others around me had no problem overcoming. But I also saw that the people around me struggled in areas that were no issue to me. That always puzzled me because I felt that if we were delivered from the power of sin and sin no longer reigned in our bodies, we should be free from all of these issues. Since then I've learned that it is not unreasonable for every man to struggle with temptation, whether in the flesh or in his spirit. The reason we don't have the same struggles is because we don't have the same history. We haven't lived through the same experiences, nor have we walked through the same wilderness. We have come from diverse cultures, traditions, and tolerances which contributed to our individual behaviors. We are equally redeemed but our journeys are quite different. It's almost impossible for anyone to accurately predict the weapon that will be most effective in causing us to disobey God. Each man is burdened with his own enticement. That is why our approach to addressing any areas of weakness should always consider the mercy of God.

I have seen faithful, dedicated believers in the body of Christ abused and rejected because they were in some area of testing, and often the problem was more hereditary then spiritual. I have seen gifted and honest men "stoned" because of some failing in their lives that caused people to see them as unsuitable for the work of God. What I saw happening in the church I knew God did not do and I didn't know how to reconcile what I was seeing with what God was saying to me about His love. There is always room for direct correction, rebuke, and loving instruction with the intent of reconciliation. Real deliverance happens in the lives of people who have allowed the process of sanctification to work its full course within them. People who have been wounded and will sometimes show no visual signs of getting better. Those in the church will have to learn how to deal with the attitudes and attacks of those who they are attempting to help. Allowing people to let down their guard and reveal their messy places in a safe area is key.

I always knew that it would be impossible to find deliverance living with places where I felt forced to cover up and hide. I knew it would take facing the problems of my life, and confronting my issues one day at a time. It came to a point where I had to be honest about my need to overcome myself and recover from some of the hurt that had me feeling bitter about the church. I had come to a point where it felt as if the people that were there to help me were the same ones who were destroying me. The church is well equipped to win men and women to Christ, but we have not yet learned how to nurture them while they are transforming into the image of Christ. Understanding this made me realize that all of the damage was not brought into the church. Some of the damage happened in the church. When we make the decision to serve God or to improve our lives in any way, we are often surprised to find that there is a gap between what we expect and what people are actually able to deliver. Never expect anyone to bring fulfillment in your life because nothing in this earth has the capacity to fulfill. Many of us are damaged because we put too much confidence in the ability of people. Let me lead you out of your fantasy Island: All men will disappoint you! All men will disappoint you and it will not be because they are trying to or because their intentions were not wholesome. It will only be because they do not have in them the ability to give you what you think they are able to give.

Expecting any man to fulfill the things in your life that you need is equivalent to seeking the living among the dead; it cannot happen. Solomon says that everything on earth is vanity and vexation of spirit. You can stop being disillusioned by people or expecting what they are not able to provide. Ultimately your healing must come from you and your trust in God's ability to take you from your crippled place to wholeness. Only God can do that. Christianity does not transform people from immaturity to maturity; weakness to strength of from struggle to victory. The key is to be able to understand and tolerate those among us who are working their way through the process.

All of my experiences are beneficial in some way. This is why God allowed me to go through so many things when it came to dealing with people. He wanted to show me that my trust could not be based in them, but only in Him. If I were able to receive help and understanding from people, then I would have to praise them. But, if I was in trouble and nobody came to my rescue then I would be more apt to declare, "If it had not been for the Lord, who was on my side I don't know where I would be." God used my experiences and even my rejections to prove His faithfulness. Sometimes God doesn't allow you to receive help from others because He wants you to be clear that He alone is your help. Despite all the things that I have faced that have challenged my destiny, I was always sure that I would one day arrive at my pre-ordained destination. God marked our lives and took the power from things that otherwise could have killed us all because He had spoken a word concerning our God-ordained purpose. The reason that you are not dead is because God has spoken a word about you that word has been sustaining your life.

In 1 Samuel 18, Saul threw the javelin at David and could not kill him because God had spoken a word over David's life. Here is the irony of the story: Saul was a Benjamite and Benjamites never missed their target. However, when Saul threw his javelin at David, the word of the Lord over David's life spoke up and said, "No, you can't kill him," and those words stood in front of David to protect him from what the enemy was throwing at him. Through all of the troubles and struggles that you have faced; you are still here. You have a mark over your life and have been chosen and separated by God. Twenty Three years ago when God told me to move to a new city to start a church, I thought, "God, I'm not ready for this. There are so many things in my life that I have not perfected; So many things that I have yet to prepare and overcome. Give me a few more years and I'll make you proud." But God was not looking for what I was going to do at some future level of maturity. He was only concerned with my availability and obedience. God is not looking for experts and professionals. He just needs somebody who is available and obedient.

I felt so inadequate that when people challenged decisions that I made, I almost agreed with them. Even though I knew that they didn't know the answers either. However, I came to understand that God never chose me because of my intellect. In fact, it had very little to do with me. God chose me because He knew I would depend on Him.

Since that time we've come through some impossible situations and have seen some incredible miracles, not by our might or power, but by the Spirit of God. God knew that we didn't mind admitting that we were incompetent to deal with situations that we had never seen before. We weren't always competent but our weakness qualified us. That was more refreshing to me than anything I had ever heard; my weakness qualified me. Perhaps this is what Paul was referring to when he talked about the pain of the thorn in his flesh. I don't pretend to know exactly what it was. However, God often brings good out of evil. He takes grievous times in our lives where we suffer and are afflicted, and work them together for our good. The design of Paul's thorn was to keep him humble, because he said, "Lest I should be exalted above measure." Paul acknowledged that he had not attained perfection. There is not much that anyone can do in order to make them perfect. Sometimes, God will allow humbling situations to make sure we realize we are not quite who we thought we were. Paul said in his second letter to the Corinthians, chapter 12 and verse 9, *"And he said unto me, my grace is sufficient for thee: for my strength is made perfect in weakness. Most gladly therefore will I rather glory in my infirmities, that the power of Christ may rest upon me."* He had never been to Corinth and yet, he planted a church in the community.

It is nearly impossible for me to adequately tell you the difficulties I had to face over these past two decades. Nor explain to you the challenges and pitfalls of getting the church off the ground; but here thereto hath the Lord helped us. Today, we see hundreds of worshippers come to the church each week. What fascinates me is not the number of people that have become a part of our church community but the fact that God uses me to lead them. All of the struggles and all those times when people abandoned left me thinking that I was not worthy. I would have never thought in a million years that God would use me. I thought I had forfeited that right a long time ago because of the multitude of rules that were presented to me.

Even though I was saved by the power of God, I had so many areas in my life that I had yet to surrender to God. I suffered from some issues for a long time and tried everything, yet still felt that I wasn't getting any better. I felt the guilt of my own inability to perfect myself before God. I felt the ridicule from those in the Christian community whose tolerance ignored the fact that though they did not have my issues, they too had a closet full of unresolved things that they never took the time to closely examine.

From the time that I was saved I wanted to please God and do all I could to obey Him. However, I was hurled into a community of believers who gave me a set of rules to follow and a list of consequences to expect as a result of failing to do so. No one in this community of believers was even fully capable of understanding my issues, nor were they interested in the dynamics that I wrestled with every day. Don't get me wrong, I do not blame anyone else for the crippled places that I've experienced in my past and even today. In fact, I've come to understand how essential they were in preparing me for the service of God. The issues I brought to the faith and the situations that led to my damages are present because I opened my life to sin and built attachments and strongholds that desired to remain, even after I made my confession of faith. I discovered that every misfortune, deliberate offense, heartache and struggle that I went through would ultimately be used for God's Glory.

There was nothing that happened to me that surprised God or caught Him off guard. For every wrong turn I made in life, He already had a planned to put me back into the right place. Every hater and cruel assailant that came in my life, only served to propel my future and push me further towards the will of God. I even consider my most ardent challenges as tools of God's intentions to perfect me. Knowing this made others appear less threatening in their methodology, rules, and opinions of what Christ desires from us as Christians.

Like the Pharisees before them they only deemed it essential that we adhere to the letter of the law and anything less would be to disobey God. Unfortunately, I was subject to their ideas for so long that I became like them and adopted their beliefs about God. I found myself being judgmental about everyone else's struggle, as though I had overcome my own. This is the part of my life I regret most. I began to feel that if God required a thing for one person, then He must be requiring it for all people. It wasn't that they didn't sin, as I discovered, but they did not recognize their own sin; which meant they could not acknowledge or understand them.

I have discovered that the areas of your greatest struggles in the world will probably be the places where you will have to fight hardest when you come into the faith. If you were selfish before you were in Christ, then you will continually struggle and war against that spirit after your conversion. If you struggled with issues of infidelity, lying, or cheating, then those will be the areas that you will most often struggle with as a believer as well until you are delivered. Of course, there are some things that through your commitment and desire to please God you will overcome right away. There will be some things that you will immediately be able to testify to that you have stopped doing after you were filled with the Holy Spirit. One of the greatest misinterpretations of the scripture is "old things are passed away, behold all things become new." When we get through quoting this scripture, a new believer is left with the fallacy that all of their problems have been immediately solved. They believed that when God delivered them from their sins, He also delivered them from their desire to sin. I must admit and I think all who read this will agree that there is a "honeymoon" with God. I call it the utopia of being saved. But when a man comes to Christ, what he really gets is a new beginning. His old desires pass away, as well as the desire to serve sin and to fulfill his own will. Everything about him becomes new. God opens what seems to be a whole new world for you, and you want to do what is necessary to be a part of that world. However, the idea of newness begins to fade as you mature in Christ. After a season, new experiences will occur that will cause you to war against new temptations and new desires. At that time it would be safe to say that, "The honeymoon is over."

There will come a time when you have to learn how to walk with God without goosebumps and without everyone celebrating you for your change. The same people who once were thanking God for you going to church, are now telling you that there are certain things you must get rid of and stop doing. By this time you will have encountered your first critic and your first hater. You may soon discover that everything is not wonderful in the church, in your life, or within yourself. Reality brings you crashing to the ground and you discover the difference between believing in and walking with God.

Am I Free?   6

I spent many years of my life as what I know to be a "broken believer." During those years I thought I just didn't want to be a Christian bad enough. I became so good at hiding my issues that I convinced myself that they weren't there. Often I felt that frustration and failure was a normal part of the saved experience. My personal fight against sin and my multiple failures in achieving that goal, coupled with the fear of admitting to those failures, took the innocence I once had and replaced it with a burden to escape. However, I thank God for His unfailing grace because I no longer view failures in my life completely in a negative light. Instead of focusing on the areas that remained unconquered, I focus on the many areas that I have overcome. Quite frankly the only negative aspect of this process was dealing with other people's reactions and expectations. The bible is replete with the stories of men and women in their battles to overcome sin. In nearly every event these people had to learn difficult and painful lessons along the way. You can't look at the lives of Moses, Noah, Jacob, David, Samson, and Peter and not be encouraged that we are men of like passions. Each of them battled weaknesses and temptations of the flesh. John writes *"In the world you shall have tribulation but be of good cheer; I have overcome the world"* (John 16:33). Please understand that wrong patterns of conduct are "second nature" to us. Behaviors such as envy, greed, lust, pride, anger, and rebellion are in all of us. Left unchecked the end result will be deceit and hostility toward God. Overcoming these will not be easy or happen overnight. It will be a life-long struggle against your carnal desires and in many cases your previous established behaviors.

When God gives us instructions to do something we strive to do it, but there is a spiritual law working against our ability to do it. In his article *How to Prevent Sin*, Herbert W. Armstrong concluded with the following: "The way to put a thing out of the mind is to put an opposite thought in the mind."

So often I have noticed parents of babies who strive to 'shush' their baby when it is crying. Usually there is either something causing pain which should be removed or the child is attempting to communicate the only way that they know how. Just saying 'shush!' or commanding the baby to stop fussing doesn't usually get very good results. Having raised children I learned the trick of quieting the baby by getting the child's mind on something other than whatever they were demanding. Instead of focusing on commanding the child to stop crying for what he or she wants, the key is to turn their attention to some new object. Change the focus and you will soon discover a cessation of the crying. Try using this same method on yourself. But instead of material or worldly things, a mature person should use self-discipline and set their minds on spiritual things. Open your bible, because by reading the word of God you will begin your journey of transforming your mind. Put the study of some spiritual subject in your mind the next time you are tempted and your flesh is screaming for its own way. Pray over your situation and ask God to help you. See how rapidly you began to win the victory over temptation and sin and how quickly your focus has changed. I have discovered that temptations will confront you all your life; they will hit you in the area of your greatest weakness and at a time when you least expect it and least prepared to resist it. You cannot assume that you are more prepared than you really are. James said, *"But every man is tempted, when he is drawn away of his own lust, and enticed. Then when lust has conceived, it brings forth sin: and sin, when it is finished, brings forth death"* (James 1:14-15).

Being broken is often beneficial if it leads to repentance and brings a greater level of humility in our lives. By definition, to be broken is to be crushed and oppressed; one Hebrew word for broken means contrite or crushed to powder. The brokenness that I have wasn't a result of my fear or reverence for God. It was a result of my frustrated response to the hopeless task of meeting the requirements that I was given by people, who told me that I couldn't be saved if I failed in any of those requirements. My way to deal with failure and broken areas was to cover those areas of broken and nakedness with the spiritual fig leaves designed to protect me from anyone seeing the real me. The leaves allowed me to avoid dealing with areas of my life that needed attention and required deliverance. It was easier to sew leaves over weak areas and cover up ugly places than to be exposed as being naked. In fact, the very fear of exposure should have been my sign that sin was present in my life, because before I was in sin I had no such concern. Genesis 2:25 says, *"And they were both naked, the man and his wife, and were not ashamed."* They had nothing to be ashamed of: They lived in a world without shame. There was complete openness before God and one another.

In Genesis Chapter 3, we are told in verses 6-8, *"When the woman say that the fruit of the tree was good for food and pleasing to the eye, and also desirable for gaining wisdom, she took some and ate it. She also gave some to her husband and he ate it. Then the eyes of both of them were opened, and they realized they were naked, so they sewed fig leaves together and made coverings for themselves. Then the man and his wife heard the sound of the Lord God as He was walking in the garden in the cool of the day, and they hid from him amongst the trees in the garden."* Imagine the openness that existed in the beginning when they were "naked and not ashamed." Now look at how things changed after man sinned; *"They sewed fig leaves together… and they hid from the Lord God…"* Sin has always been the basis for our desire to hide from each other and cover up those unattractive things about ourselves and avoid communion with God. In fact, many of us fail to go forward in life because we are afraid to expose what we think nobody knows about us or maybe the fear of highlighting what we think they do know about us. So then what is real freedom all about?

Living Behind the Mask   7

I grew up in Saraland, Alabama, a small town far north of Mobile, Alabama. Nothing can diminish my love of all those experiences that I had while living there. I don't have any unpleasant memories of those times, even though they were laced with some unhappy situations. I can't say that I didn't have some personal battles. But they were largely a result of how society viewed me and other blacks living in the deep south. Some of it was perhaps due to my lack of focus and commitment to be successful despite my surroundings. As I look back on it, growing up in the sixties were prominent in everyone's memory that had to live through them. The blatant racism that was present and the hatred and inequities in the schools, coupled with the class and color struggle within our own race, made being black a challenging obstacle. Yes, in those days there were obvious internal battles within the black community which suggested that a person was not as attractive if your skin was of a darker complexion. Even whites felt that if you had a lighter complexion you were "less black." Fortunately, I was raised in a home that made that less of an issue than black people was making out of it. My mother and father had a good sense of who they were and worked very hard to shield us from the racism of the south and the lack of self-awareness in our own community. They instilled within my siblings and me so much confidence that I learned to defy the stereotypes within my own race. God gave me parents who had a healthy sense of their worth and pushed that in me. They taught me that it was alright to try and even acceptable to fail. I was taught to never be ashamed of who I was and never try to become who I was not. Those lessons made me who I am today and I will be forever thankful for them. I later learned how critical having that information would be to my life.

Mobile was a city of the real and the imagined. Every year in February nearly every citizen and former citizen of Mobile began to convene downtown for the two week festival that we call Mardi Gras. For those of you who are socially challenged, Mardi Gras is a French Carnival celebration which culminates following Fat Tuesday. The participants eat the last night of fatty foods before the start of the ritual fasting during the Lentel season. There were all kinds of parades throughout the downtown area, private balls, packed streets, and merriment throughout the city. One of the things that I used to love about Mardi Gras was the colorful costumes and masks that people wore as part of the celebration. For a long time, I wondered why the costumes and masks were worn and wondered about their significance. Later I discovered that the costumes were part of the fantasy of Mardi Gras, because they allowed the wearer to be a part of the Mardi Gras tradition of role reversal. The wearer could conceal their identity and parody authority figures in society. They would mock clergy or even the educated. I found this interesting because instead of being yourself, Mardi Gras was a time when you could pretend to be someone else. So, I started thinking, is the church operating in a continual Mardi Gras season, where fantasy and parody is more accepted than reality? It certainly appears that way when so many believers feel pressured to wear a mask and pretend to be someone they can never be. By wearing "costumes" that are designed to present an image of a person that they are not, all for the benefit of the crowd. Perhaps when you put the mask on it becomes difficult to remove it because we find that so many people accept it. The idea of concealing ones true identity is popular and seems preferable in the church. What a terrible way to be forced to live, hiding your true self and taking on the image of someone else. The danger of this cover up is that it never allows you to do the real work of becoming what you need to be because you have found that it is acceptable to pretend to be someone else.

Another reason I believe people wear masks in the church is because it may be the only way they feel safe. They may feel that by covering themselves they can avoid the condemnation brought on by those who would condemn them instead of restoring them. As a teenager, I recall working at a shipyard that built really large battle ships for the military. As part of the safety requirements while working as a welders apprentice, I had to wear a face shield. I remember how uncomfortable it made me because I couldn't see or hear anything except the beam from the weld. That face shield was designed to protect me from the danger of welding balls that would randomly land and the flash of weld blindness that occurred from direct contact with the eye from focusing on the welding gun. I eventually got accustomed to being uncomfortable and accepted it as a necessary part of working for the company.

Maybe this is why so many people in the church continue to wear their mask, because it feels like it is part of their safety equipment. For many years I only felt accepted by covering up, and never exposing anyone to my true self. I would work and constantly cover myself from the danger of of being exposed as not being perfect. Often when you find yourself pleasing people you are probably not pleasing God. Nobody really wanted to know my truths except those who desired to take advantage of my failures. What kind of love system is it that makes it unacceptable to be yourself and force you to hide the fact that godly living is a process that each of us are working on and few of us are good at?

One of the most confusing terms that I heard in the church was the term "Come as you are." What does that really mean and how many churches that say it really mean it? I always felt that this concept is biblically based but poorly applied by too many churches and believers. This term spoke to me of the grace of God offered to those who had no right to God. Now the the beauty of the gospel of Jesus Christ is that anybody who came to Him, He would in no wise cast out and whosoever calls on the name of the Lord, they shall be saved. This felt like God loved me as the individual I was and not as the person others wanted me to be or forced me to pretend I was.

Sometimes well-meaning Christians give people the impression that they must surrender some of the sins of their lives before Jesus will accept them and if He accepts them they must immediately rid themselves of any error in their lives on their own. I'm often reminded of the woman at the well who had been married five times and now she was living with a man she was not married to (John 14:1-26). Although Jesus addressed her condition, He offered her salvation and not just change. This is a good point because it is not necessary to ignore sin, but it is critical that we offer salvation from the sin but not as a prerequisite to be saved. This leads me back to one of my basic premises that we cannot cleanse ourselves and our need of God is not to get us to be holy through our works, but through the grace He has offered us. The church has proven invaluable at doing feel good things that are worthy, but may not be the weightier part, such as feeding the homeless, paying utility bills and rent, clothing the naked and addressing injustices in society. But what happens when divorcees, gay people, known fornicators, strippers come through the church door? It's not hard to find people who like the woman in John 14 find the church not to be a friendly place when it comes to cultivating a relationship with God. There is a big difference in how somebody who is accepted by society feels when coming into a church, only to find that their lifestyle is not acceptable. We talk about the work of the church and evangelism, but most of the time we don't have the stomach for evangelism, or the heart for those we say we want to evangelize. Our expectations for the most part are not realistic. We want them to go through their process by next week and never go back to any of the sins of their previous life. We tend to view any failure as a disappointment to us, and an embarrassment to God. We want to add to the church daily, while determining who is being added. In some cases, we are no different from some of the new converts. While we are offended and disgusted over their issues, we are simply overlooking the fact that we all have issues. How can we cast ourselves to be the judge in any scene or storyline? We have "all sinned and fallen short of the glory of God." While we fight over the semantics of that claim, it doesn't change it. Not one of us can be justified in God based on our merit. We need to stop splitting straws or seeing ourselves as better when all of us are the same. We are sinners who just happen to have different flavors of sin. I often have had a problem with the disgust of someone who can tolerate a "saved" person who is a fornicator, but is unable to deal with one being a gossiper. The bible clearly tells us to *"cleanse ourselves of the filthiness of the soul and spirit, perfecting holiness in the fear of God"* (2 Cor 7:1). The aforementioned scripture is saying to us that we all have some work to be done.

One of the things I observe is that people who have overcome areas in their flesh often still have work to do because they have to fight the spirits of gossip and judgment. These spirits will make one think of themselves more highly than you ought. The goal for all of us is to be clean both inside and out.

As believers we sometimes live in fear of what might happen to us if someone from our church fellowship or faith community discovers some ugly truth about us. This is like spending too much of our time trying to convince dirt that it is dirt. When all of us are men of like passion and varied issues but equally revealing. We all suffer from some weakness or propensity that has the potential of leading us to sin. We all have been guilty of falling to some areas of sin, whether by the commission or by omission, and we all struggle to stop. How dare we approach each other with some sanctimonious air when we are quite aware of our own failings. Who are we trying to fool? It's not fair to believers who are trying their best to develop a relationship with God under such scrutiny and the false assumption that the people who they see as examples of godly men and women are without faults.

It became a discouraging and impossible feat in my journey to godliness and I am sure I am not alone. Again, I'm not trying to give freedom to sinful behavior. But I am saying that after 20 years of serving God, I acknowledge that I still have struggles. However, I will encourage others that the journey of perfection has to be travelled one day at a time. The first step to healing damaged places in our lives is in our willingness to expose our nakedness and at least make people aware of the coverings we've made for ourselves. God already knows who we are and it is a waste of time trying to convince Him or others that we are who we pretend to be. He would rather you confess your present condition, admit and acknowledge your sins, and come spiritually naked before Him so that He can help you cope with the scars of being damaged. When we look at Genesis 2:25, the word used to define nakedness is similar to being without covering or clothing. In Genesis 3, the word that we see is *empty, void* and *nothing*. In other words, what Adam told God was, I hid from you because I knew that I was unfit, ashamed, and insufficient. This is a powerful admission and it speaks to the truth of our lives because we have been so ever since Adam. It is not until we realize our inability to fix certain things in our lives that we will ever be able to say we are ready to face God. We will never be able to face God if we are not ready to face ourselves.

There are a lot of reasons for Moses' reluctance to go before Pharaoh. Consider the fact that God was calling Moses to go back to a land where he was still a fugitive, wanted for murder and he saw his own safety as being threatened. This story is found in Exodus 2, where we see that one day Moses went out and saw an Egyptian beating a Hebrew, one of his own people. He then kills the Egyptian and buries him in the sand thinking that he was not seen. But the next day he went out and saw two Egyptians fighting and asked them why they were fighting. One of them said, "Who made you judge over us, are you going to kill me like you killed my fellow Hebrew?" You see, just because you didn't see anyone while you were doing whatever you were doing does not mean they did not see you. Fear came upon Moses as he discovered that his sin was not hidden. Moses began his futile journey to escape the penalty of sin; much like many of us who think that running far enough from it is the answer to overcoming it. But in Exodus 3, God is sending him back. It was an impossible task in his mind to return to the scene of the crime and command his pursuers not only to let him go, but to free every Israelite slave.

The problem was Moses looked at his own abilities rather than God's mighty ability to use him. He clearly had cognitive challenges, because we are told that he was concerned that he would not be able to match Pharaoh's wisdom and his excellence of speech. "O my Lord, I am not eloquent, neither before nor since you have spoken to your servant; but I am slow of speech and slow of tongue." God replied, "Who made your mouth? And who makes some deaf, some blind and some to see. Now go and do as I have told you, I will help you speak well and I will tell you what you are to say." Some of us need to know that God sees our problems and will give us on- the- job-training. He made you the way that you are and when He calls you, (though you feel inadequate or insufficient) He will give you the ability to articulate, perform, and fully carry out His plans with excellence. Today Moses would have been considered to suffer from low self-esteem and a lack of confidence in himself and God. He said, "Who am I to appear before Pharaoh? If I go to the people of Israel and tell them, the God of your ancestors has sent me to you, they won't believe me, they will ask, 'Which god are you talking about? What is His name?', and then what should I tell them?"

Too many people suffer from underestimating the

power of God and miss the fact that the call of God never depends on your ability but His ability. When you complain about your appearance, your abilities, or your aptitude to be successful in God, you are really questioning the power of God. God wants to do a mighty work in us, but that can't happen if we make it all about us. We have to stop underestimating the power of God and begin to understand that He is bigger than all of our problems, situations, and dilemmas.

My search to know the will of God has brought me to unexpected areas and through some "valleys of the shadow of death." I have spent a good deal of time in my early days of faith trying to understand how to reconcile the rhetoric of religion (often heard in the testimonies of God's people) with the reality of everyday living. I have struggled with seeing believers who undoubtedly love God ridiculed and shunned in the house of faith because they fail to meet the recognized expectations or violate the established behavior of the church.

My problem lies in the apparent hypocrisy involved with such a system, because it often speaks to personal weaknesses and cultural taboos. It would be interesting to somehow count the number of people who were driven from the fellowship of the church because they failed to conform to the established norms or struggled beyond the allotted time of man's grace. I wonder if we would find them serving God somewhere else or living with bitterness, hurt, and anger; damaged from the church's failure to allow them to discover their place in the kingdom before rushing them out of the door.

What are these believers doing about their own shortcomings while condemning others about their imperfections? The truth is that even the most connected believer suffers from the same temptations and desires of sin.

Stop Pretending 8

The church is one entity that exists in every society. There are a few places you can travel in this world and not find a church. However, one question that has to be answered is, "Why is the church here, and how does it still stand when many institutions and nations have failed to continue to exist?" The church has played a major role in society, where it provides an eternal order in which many people resolve in believing that they will attain salvation through its teaching. Many people turn to the church for solace and refuge from the harsh reality of the world, since it is known to provide hope and comfort. However, in an article written by L. Sally, *Experiences of Social Exclusion at Home and Church Environments*, we are told that with the dynamism of society this is not entirely the case. In the opinion of most individuals within society, the church does not offer this comfort anymore. The main reason may relate to the societal pressure of having to pretend to fit in within church fellowships. This is true in nearly all congregations and arises mainly from various reasons, such as the role society plays in peoples' lives, or the fear of judgment and rejection. There are many embedded reasons why people tend to succumb to the pressure of pretence and false representation. One should ask, "Is there a long term emotional or psychological impact on a person that results from feeling pressured to be perfect.

There are many people within society who tend to pretend whenever they get into a church setting, since the goal for many of them is to gain acceptance within the church congregation. Despite the fact that the church is considered as a place where everyone is welcome, this does not apply to everyone. There are various reasons why people seek the solace and refuge of the church. Most people think and feel that they do not belong within a particular setting. While in certain arenas everybody is perceived to be righteous because of their imperfections. As a result, many believers feel it is necessary to conceal their flaws instead of confronting them or be honest about them. The various choices and actions they have made within life have made them feel as though they are not worthy to be what they think everyone else is. So many will only resort to choosing a life of pretense within the church in order to feel accepted. It is only human for people to want association with others and be accepted and recognized despite their former actions and choices.

Other people, on the other hand, will feel a need to pretend and be what they are not in order to impress people within society. Societal settings and ideologies have led people to be divided greatly into various factions. For example, society considers the rich as powerful and influential people who are always showered with praise and attention. In the church setting for instance, one would choose a life of pretense in order to be associated with certain factions within the church, or in order to have influence and attention[1]. Associations with some groups within the church lead people to want to be linked to them in order to be noticed, as well as impress the clergy and congregation. Unfortunately, this postmodern church is often more interested in celebrities than in Christ. As a result, the rules of standards of each group that you might connect with may be more focused on social status, economics, or appearance than faith. This can be a challenge for some young believers who see the church as a place where they can find fellowship and support.

Despite the fact that the church is a place where one finds solace, peace and refuge from the harsh and cruel world, most people will not feel its warmth and comfort. In today's society, the church has changed from a place of worship to a place where people meet and talk about their daily lives. It poses a difficult setting for people whose lives have not quite worked out, and they tend to feel and consider themselves as misfits within the church. Therefore, it prompts them to adopt a life of pretense in order for them to fit within the congregation and to have a sense of belonging within the church. It brings about a different setting within the church that is not supposed to be there in

[1] Goodemann, C. (2012). The Wolf In Sheep's Clothing: church members Veiled as Innocent. *Trends And Resources*, 124-127.

the first place.[2]

Some people choose a life of pretense especially within the church, since they want recognition within the church environment. They do not want to show their real personalities, faults or vulnerability sine they want to come out as an interesting person. Recognition comes about with the impression of the human environment and the main motivation for this is that they would not like to feel secluded. It would also have come about with the individual's reasons to achieve aspects of self-actualization and ultimate attention within the church setting. It prompts people to choose a life of pretense within the church setting in order for them to gain the ultimate respect and recognition they think they deserve despite the harsh reality and facts that life brings about[3].

Most people tend to live a life of pretense within the church because they are not entirely secure with their status and lack self-confidence. Others may choose this way of life in order for them to attain their goals and achievements within the church. With a "good" reputation, manipulation is easy amongst the congregants. Most of these people will tend to use this to their advantage and elevate their status to

[2] Sally, L. (2012). Experiences Of Social Exclusison at home and church environments. *social and religious studies*, 101-109.

[3] Gravdal, L. (2010). Church Members experiences of being presured- And How They Envisage Their Dream Day. *Caring Sciences*, 791-798.

the top of the congregation and within the church setting[4]. It brings about one of the main reasons why people choose to live a life of pretense within the church in order for them to get their achievements through improper ways.

Some of the people within various church congregations will tend to live a life of pretense since they themselves have no idea who they really are. As mentioned earlier, most subjects will try to gain recognition within the society thus live lives that are not theirs. They would like to emulate certain figures in society since they have already made it in life and get all the attention they deserve. For them not to feel excluded, the only way to achieve this is to adopt this particular way of life[5]. Most of these people do not want to face reality and would use any excuse to claw their way in life, and prefer to lie to themselves into a better existence.

The lack of self-confidence and belief in oneself will make most people adopt a life of pretense in order for them to fit within society. Most of these people tend to think that the congregation or society in general will judge and seclude them since they have not made it in life. The fear of their true identity and character being judged prompts them to adopt various personas. This reasoning causes them to desire to fit in with certain church members to cover up feelings of being unworthy and unimportant. According to

---

[4] Liu, J. (2011). Adult pressures: A Review Of Constructs, Concepts And church Implications. *Public Health Nursing*, 556-568.

[5] Gravdal, L. (2010). Church Members experiences of being presured- And How They Envisage Their Dream Day. *Caring Sciences*, 791-798.

Carol Goodemann, who is the author of *"The Wolf in Sheep's Clothing: Church Members Veiled as Innocent"* fear of being rejected is the main reason why most people choose this kind of life.

Sometimes people are embarrassed and that often results in pretending to make themselves feel better. It often comes about with the idolization of prominent people in church in order to make their self-worth feel elevated. Many people do not want to accept their status in life, their faults or their poor choices they have made. They may have various psychological and emotional consequences, such as being stigmatized and left out. Thus the main reason why people would choose a life of pretense is to avoid these factors and consequences from society. In addition, they would want to feel as if they are important within society and the church in general.

Most people tend to live lives of pretense if they are ashamed of themselves and their past actions. Some of these choices have had severe consequences and outcomes that have completely changed their image and reputation. I know a lot about this because of my own failures and problems along with the pressure I felt from possible exposure.

I can remember being crippled at the possible loss of my reputation and status. Most people will turn to fake personas and lives of pretention in order to cover all the actions of their past. Eventually, it all comes down to them attempting to avoid being judged and secluded from other congregants.

In a home or church setting, people may often feel the

urge to pretend that they are perfect so that they can be loved as well as encouraged by their peers. Everyone faces troubles and challenges. Many individuals find it difficult to be able to deal with the problems that they face. They feel the need to seek out places where they receive love, support and encouragement. Often these places of comfort include home and church environments. As a result, a majority of them may feel that the church is full of righteous people and they will not be accepted based on their true identities. They may end up feeling deprived of the love and encouragement that they are seeking. It can be conclusively said that pretense in the home environment is often so that the persons can receive love and encouragement without the fear of being judged.

For the Christians that have the intention to promote the gospel, some have a need to pretend to be perfect in the eyes of the rest of the congregation. There is an assumption that if persons are not "holy" and pure, then they will not be setting the perfect example for the congregation to follow. They may feel the pressure to pretend to be a perfect role model. Furthermore, they have the duty to preach. Perhaps the gospel that they wish to promote will not be accepted if they lived a different lifestyle. The main aim of preaching would be to gather disciples and tell the good news about the crucifixion resurrection and of Jesus Christ. It is a classic example of preaching water and drinking wine. Hence one would need to assume the "perfect image."

Some people who are expected to be "perfect" often show symptoms of depression. Previous studies show that depressed individuals are likely to get affected by pressure that they have submitted to by society. Various studies have proved that the individuals studied have produced shallow findings but there is a presence in the relationship between church going and depression in the clinical studies and the overall population samples.

There had been ongoing discussions to relate depression with the need to be perfect and other emotional and psychological disorders. A causal relationship has been established between the two, making the assumption that when an individual is faced with reasons to be perfect in a church or home setting, they go into depression. The beginning or identification of other psychological disorders may be greatly affected by fear of psychological, emotional, and physical pressure, isolation, shaming the family or church. These are some of the reasons which make a person prone to psychological, emotional, and physical pressure. It has been suggested that those common symptoms usually are caused by conflict within an individual. It is present especially in young children who are entering their teenage years. Most of these teenage children are always focused on establishing relationships, which are often intimate with their peers either in church or at home.

People may have a different perspective when it comes to comparing themselves to the standards of the society and the church. Even the person's life may be good and noteworthy; they may still have the need to pretend to be perfect in order for them to fit into the higher ideals that are set by the society. In reality, no one in the church is perfect and they are all pretending. Nonetheless, it is essential for people to have insight into the differences in cognition and perception to enable them to cope with the pressures of such social environments. The people who often give in to the pressure of the need to be perfect have limited cognitive abilities and they lack the necessary skills to deal with the changes found in church processes [6]. Many people tend to be very egocentric and blame themselves for their troubling lives, and worse they may feel it is their responsibility to live up to the definitions of society. Some people are at times needy emotionally and crave for acceptance.

Another major factor is reduced self-esteem. Psychological, emotional, and physical pressure are a few risk factors of feeling the need to be perfect. It has been further suggested that the possibility of rejection by peers may result in the misinterpretation of various social events. A perfect example would be if a person is depressed and has a negative self-concept. There is the possibility of them perceiving others in the church or home as rejecting them. They may consider and interpret other persons to be hostile, and may sense this in social interactions advanced by other persons during fellowship.

Some people may not accept the circumstances as they are and may have fantasies about reconciling the church and

---

[6] Sally, L. (2012). Experiences Of Social Exclusison at home and church environments. *social and religious studies*, 101-109.

their peers. However, they are less likely to hold themselves responsible for their troubling past. They may experience intense grief for not living up to the pre-established standards. For persons that have learned to cope with the pressure, they may be more capable of explaining and expressing their disappointment and to be able to show who they really are. They may be very aware of the anger that some of their peers feel towards them.

Studies go on to suggest that social skills and the ability to defend themselves are impaired in persons that feel they have to hide their troubling backgrounds. Due to these reasons they have become easy prey and targets for "holier than thou" people. It can be concluded that victimization and depression in the church impairs social skills. People who are "victimized" are considered submissive, and always are thought to behave in a helpless manner. These people display reduced self-esteem. All the above named patterns and tendencies have the potential to expose them to psychological, emotional, and physical pressure and antecedents of depression.

Studies show that "holier than thou" people externalize antisocial tendencies such as manipulation, overt aggression, and lack of empathy. Peer groups in the church and at home have always known to have a great deal of pressure and influence on the "perfect" behaviors. Expression of a person's troubled past may be one of the major factors of subjectivity within peer groups. People who are more popular in society, church, or within their family have been found to be more socially responsive and fit into all societal standards. Their ability to fit into certain standards is used to influence other individuals in order to maintain a certain social status within their peer groups.

As mentioned earlier, low self-esteem usually associated with victimization has been rejected recently by studies which suggest there is no relationship between self-esteem and church going, or raised self-esteem and the "holier than thou" people. The "I am perfect image" has been linked with the need to control others. The need to hide one's past has been associated with the previous absence of self-control. It is present from previous studies, which have shown that the "holier than thou" people are always considered to have higher levels of social intelligence with comparison to their peers.

The teenage population demonstrated a higher association between psychological, emotional, and physical pressure from church going, according to various cases entailing depression that were self-reported in the various cross sectional surveys. A large number of people that were pretenders were considered to be dissatisfied with their own lives.

Within a variety of stigmatized and victimized people, was a risk factor among them. It was seen that people that suffered from imperfect pasts were more likely to be victimized in a number of ways, with the addition of rejection within their lives, compared to those that did not have any troubling past[7].

Studies showed that the need to be accepted in the church or home, which lasted for a longer duration of time or was more intense, left the victims exposed to depression. In the adults that had been victims of anxiety disorders, there was a high association between depression and other social impairments and functional anxiety. Other studies revealed a history of rejection and isolation in the home or church due to a troubled past. These behaviors were tied to suicide, even after the persons left the church or home.

Other research suggested that social skills and the ability to defend oneself are often impaired in people who fear being rejected. As a result, they become easy targets for "holier than thou" people. He concluded that the psychological, emotional, and physical pressure in people weakens social skills. People who are the victims of rejection and isolation have been found to be submissive, and behave in a helpless manner, and are considered less popular by their peers. These people display reduced self-esteem. All these above named patterns and tendencies have the potential to expose them to psychological, emotional, physical pressure and depression.

Prior research done on the pre-adolescent population showed that psychological, emotional, and physical pressures were related to several psychosomatic symptoms

---

[7] Rueger, S. (2014). Effects Of Peer Victimistataion On Psychological And Social Adjustments In Earlry Adolescence. *American Psychological Association*, 77-88.

and depressions in persons that felt that they needed to pretend for them to be accepted. Rejection in the church was seen to have a direct prediction on the severity of the depression that they suffered, especially for the females. Liu established that acceptance in the church and home of those children was a predetermining component of being hospitalized in psychiatric facilities. It was also instrumental in the use of antidepressants or antipsychotics as early as 25 years old, to regulate the psychopathologies.

When the literature attained is analyzed, a contradiction arises at some dimension. The literature suggests that there is a strong association between psychological, emotional, and physical pressure, and the need to be perfect in church is variant when it comes to gender differences. Some research has highlighted the potential to lead to higher chances of depression in men. Depression was considered to be one of the risk factors for the development of psychological, emotional, and physical pressure of women. There has been research that has come forward to highlight that the relationship between bio-psycho-social pressure and depression is more preset in women, rather than men. The findings of the research highlight that depression is a major antecedent for psychological, emotional, and physical pressure especially for men. Persons that fail to conform to the standards of society as defined by the church and the home are more likely to develop depression.

Research that was analyzed confirms the fact that there is the possibility of psychological, emotional, and physical pressure arising in persons that suffer from damaged self-perception. One of the possible reasons for this is that as persons enter into the church; their confidence is founded on the type of relationships that they will cultivate. If the focus of the people was to be on more important areas, such as fellowship and worship, then there are chances that the people would not give such sentimental value to the relationships that they foster with other people. A highlight of the literature is that it confirms that there is a high correlation between church going and pretense in individuals. Those who feel they need to pretend, or be accepted displayed symptoms of depression. Retrospective studies have suggested that psychological, emotional, and physical pressure, because of pretending to be perfect is a risk factor when it comes to depression. Those individuals that are depressed are more prone to suicidal tendencies. Studies on clinically referred individuals are shallow but suggest that there is a relationship between depression and pretending in the clinical, as well as the population samples.

A critical look at the literature used has unveiled another eminent shortcoming. The literature failed to take into consideration that there may be other preexisting conditions which would serve as a facilitator for the development of the need to pretend, despite the fact that the child has been a victim of pressure in the church or in the home. The factors are inclusive of the medical condition that may be present prior to the situation, such as bipolar disorders or other facilitating conditions such as conflict and frustration. The existence of these conditions may push the person to feel they need to pretend to be perfect.

It can also be argued that for those that go to church, they have no reason to pretend. The church is the ideal place for them to show who they really are, and they will be accepted. The church is somewhere people go to seek forgiveness. Sinners are welcomed to repent and seek forgiveness when they believe. Christians believe that the church is where the sinners can be offered forgiveness, and the sinner can be given guidance on how they can live in a way that is right in the eyes of the society. It is for this reason that it can be argued that a person would not feel the pressure to hide who they are. They tend to think that they will be encouraged to reveal their true selves as they seek to be offered forgiveness.

The argument can also be applied in the home setting, such that the person should not feel the pressure to hide who they are. Instead they should be encouraged to reveal their true selves. Often a home environment is nurturing and encourages one to grow. One cannot be judged in the home or be criticized. They will be embraced and welcomed into the home when they reveal who they are, without the fear of violation or isolation. As a result, one would not feel the need to pretend among other persons.

God Accepts All of You 9

THe fact that God accepts all of us should be good to know. It doesn't change God's desire for change in you, but He accepts and loves all of you. If you have ever been rejected by people because of the way they perceived you or valued you, then you know how devastating rejection feels. The pressure of not being accepted can and has been crippling to a lot of people. However, rejection is not all that uncommon in a number of settings. Acceptance by God begins with an understanding of what God did so that He could accept you. His only Son, Jesus, was sacrificed on the cross as the payment for your sins. Without the atonement at the cross of Calvary, God could not accept sinners like us. However, through Christ, we are accepted by the Father. When you accept Jesus Christ into your life you are automatically separated from the world. Those who are not yet believers may find it difficult to understand the mindset of someone who has been saved from their sins. But for those of us who were accepted, when we know that we didn't deserve to be received into Christ's love, will always be grateful and humbled by the love showed to us through Jesus. Can you imagine the devastation of having given your only son to save someone and they think that they can take care of things for themselves?

In Matthew 15, we see the story of a woman who was a Canaanite; a Syrian Phoenician to be exact, who were known as ancestral enemies of the Jews. They occupied Palestine from times before Abraham. These were the descendants of Ham, that Noah had cursed to be enslaved to his brother Shem. They were such heathens and idol worshippers, that God commanded the Jews not to mingle with them at all. They were looked at with disgust. Because of their reputations, the Jews could have no dealings with them. However, the Bible states that this particular woman had a need. Her daughter was possessed by demons and she wanted her to be free of the demonic power. It is behind this backdrop that we find that despite her race, culture, reputation, or condition, her need led her to Jesus. One of the most tragic things taking place in the world today is for people to discover their needs, but refuse to come to Jesus.

The greatest reason to toil and labor with people who we would have normally been rejected, is because of their need for Jesus. We should respond to their desperation because someone responded to ours. When you have a real need, it won't matter who fulfills it. You will look past protocol, what people have done or what they think about you in order to have your need met. So often, the people who have come to us have already walked an extra mile. I've seen people treated poorly while standing in line at the welfare office without concern of others overhearing their conversations, just to have a need addressed. This is how I have come to understand that when you have a real need, you will cover up your pride and ask, even though you stand the chance of being insulted.

Allow me first to digress from my point, and say that fewer people are coming to church as if they have a need. We live in a day where church has become just one of the options that people enjoy. It is certainly not the only option and not even the only spiritual option anymore. There is no sense of desperate anticipation of God's presence in our churches or in our lives and we are left with the routine obligation of being present instead of the privilege of being allowed to come in. We have filled our rooms with spectators and we miss our chance of seeing God because of the distraction of seeing each other. This is the most tragic part of our "routine" church services. While we are talking about seeking the presence of God, all too often we miss God. We are more moved by seniority in the pew, and unless something extraordinary happens, we never move nor do we acknowledge the privilege of just being there. We watch others praise God while we sit idle, like He's not our God too.

The events of this world have become so life threatening, that we can no longer afford to be entertained during the times when we come together to worship. We do not need church services that mask the realities that each believer lives when they are not at church. What we really need is the kind of worship that will bring deliverance to the lives of those who stumble into the grace of God because of His call. We need worshippers who will not be as concerned with each other's violation as they are God's presence. Our churches have made the mistake of reprioritizing church to the point that worship has become subject to our schedule. In most church settings it has become more and more difficult to see real deliverance or genuine repentance, because of the confines we have placed on God to move within our "worship hour." As a result, how are we going to influence freedom among those in this world when there is no sense of unity, wholeness, freedom, or healing in the church? Contrary to the critics, the presence of God is not hindered as much by the disobedience of people, as it is by the judgmental attitude that proceeds them. What we really need is a people who are willing to make worship real in their own lives and a people who will be more concerned with working out their own salvation than overwhelmed about if others are working out theirs or not. This kind of worship will disrupt heaven and cause God to forgive sins and heal our land.

We should come to God with such desperation that it forces us to run to him, grab hold of the horns of the altar, and remain there until we are able to stand around a death bed while declaring "It's not over." We should be able to speak to dead marriages and declare them to recover; and decree supernatural breakthroughs in the finances of people who are willing to believe. There is without question a power shortage in the church and I don't know if our best practice should surround picking out the imperfection of others or judging their sincerity. What we need to do is obey the command of God to love one another and by doing so we fulfill the law of God. We should also always remember that Satan has and will forever be an accuser of the brethren and that means we should not be surprised that he would try and pull your focus to the sins and inconsistencies of fellow believers. It is his job to point out the violations of people who claim to be free.What he doesn't understand is that our perfection is not based on our deeds but on Christ's works. Paul wrote in Galatians that *"Christ hath redeemed us from the curse of the law, being made a curse for us...*(Galatian 3:13). Even when you know that the devil is knocking you to the right and to the left with accusations about your character and your commitment, you should remind yourself that Christ's redemptive power is at work in your life. Even in those times when your deeds are proof of his accusation, keep reminding yourself that Christ has redeemed us from the curse of the law. We cannot redeem ourselves. When we can do that, then our church experiences will be powerful and we will see what we have missed. It is in that environment of Pentecost that was spoken of in Acts 2 will revisit the church again. *"And when the day of Pentecost was fully come, they were all with one accord in one place. And suddenly there came a sound from heaven as of a rushing mighty wind, and it filled all the house where they were sitting. And there appeared unto them cloven tongues like as of fire, and it sat upon each of them. And they were all filled with the Holy Ghost, and began to speak with other tongues, as the Spirit gave them utterance."* We need a divine visitation that has been missing in our churches but we will never have it until we get on one accord in one place. We will never have it by exalting each other's faults, tendencies and imperfections. We will get there by celebrating the things that make the whole body of Christ complete.

It's time for us to get violent and show the world, especially those who have given up on the church, that we can be one. The church has spent too many years held back because we have tried to be what we are not. Perhaps we didn't understand that God didn't call us to fit in but to take over. When will you learn to accept the value of your uniqueness and stop insisting on defining your dedication to God by conforming to the dictates of man? Though it makes us more comfortable in our surroundings, it doesn't breathe the purposes of God. We seek fellowships where we connect culturally, racially, socio-economically, rather than finding the one that meets our deeper need.

Many believers have become frustrated because there are so many proclaimed church experts defining God's will for them. These believers have lost their burning passion for their faith and service to God because of the requirements of men. As a result, that fire has given way to complacency and routine. People are literally unaware of the authority they could have in God and the joy of serving God because of all of these doctrinal roadblocks that is keeping them from knowing who God really is. I call them "silly church games" because we spend valuable time going through the motions and giving examples of what we should and shouldn't do. Instead of lifting people they are left with a watchdog mentality of God and Christianity that makes it very difficult to adhere to. God has a way of inviting Himself into the lives of people who are not a part of the "in" crowd and into the lives of those who have been rejected or not a part of the clique. He has sensitivity to people who are outsiders, aliens, underprivileged, and displaced. Much of the Old Testament record is filled with men and women who were considered underdogs. He took those who were thrown into the valley of the shadow of death, and used them for His glory. In Luke 7, we are given the story of a woman who was a prostitute that had come into Simon's house to wash Jesus' feet. Luke tells us that Simon was a Pharisee. The Pharisees often had an antagonistic relationship with Jesus, but they were in some ways the ones who kept the integrity of the law and ensured that the intent of God was communicated with the people. There were four major sects of Pharisees and all of them had an identity resulting from their experiences, but they all were a result of the successful Maccabean Revolt that led to religious freedom for the Jews and subsequent power. Therefore, by the time of Jesus these group of pious and separated men were the powers in the Jewish community and they were to be recognized as such.

Simon, though inviting Jesus to his house, didn't do so to honor Jesus but to be mock him. Evident by the fact that he never extended to him the customary recognitions offered to an honored guest of washing of their hands and feet, oil poured over their head, and the traditional kiss on the cheek. His real objective was (as in most cases) to have Jesus seen as less than authoritative and prophetic being.

However, in comes this woman with a jar of oil, who fell at the feet of Jesus washing his feet with her tears and drying them with her hair. She showed him the honor that Simon did not by pouring the expensive oil on his feet and kissed them. If only the church would learn how to demonstrate God to those who everyone does not honor.

God has never been concerned with who is the most popular. He delights in the humble and the contrite and uses the least popular for His purpose. He does it in order for it to be clearly understood that when the miracle comes, men will know beyond a shadow of a doubt that it is not a result of status or position, but it is by the power of God. He did it. It is time to stand still and watch God move. The next time you get in the midst of something and realize that you are overmatched, try this: instead of crying and complaining about the situation, start shaking heaven with praise and prayer until God gives you victory. Your victory is not in your belief alone, but it lies in the power of God. This means that it may not come today, but you have to keep believing until it happens. It will happen.

I celebrate God's willingness to use who nobody else thinks is usable and He does it to confound the wise. I have lost a number of relationships because I chose to stand in the liberty of God opposed to the traditions of men. I was told that I was guilty of compromise and that I was somehow leaving the truth of God's word. As a result of it, I would without a doubt not be saved. I have gone from being celebrated in some areas to being ostracized and labeled, but it led me on a journey unlike any I have undertaken before. I no longer chase the approval of man, but my hunger came to chase after the approval of God. I went from thinking I knew what God required, to being forced into a process of forgetting all of that and asking God to teach me His way all over again. This led me to understand that relationship with God is about grace. Now I have talked about grace, but I don't think you really understand grace until you recognize your need for grace. With so many years of faithful service and faithful dedicated ministry to a group, I was now forced to ask the question, "Did I know God or did I know the GOD of the group?"

Delivered But 10

A gain, I want to talk about the biblical story of Mephibosheth because, for me, it displays a perfect example of a person who had been damaged by life but God turned it around and caused a blessing to come from his life. In 2 Samuel 9, David said, *"Is there still anyone who is left of the house of Saul, that I may show him kindness for Jonathan's sake?" And there was a servant of the house of Saul whose name was Ziba. So when they called him to David, the king said to him, "Are you Ziba?" He said, "At your service!" Then the king said, 'Is there not still someone of the house of Saul to whom I may show the kindness of God?' And Ziba said to the king, "There is still a son of Jonathan who is lame in his feet." So the king said to him, "Where is he?" and Zaiba said to the king, "Indeed he is in the house of Machir, the son of Ammiel, in Lo Debar." Then King David sent and brought him out of the house of Machir, the son of Ammiel, from Lo Debar. Now when Mephibosheth the son of Jonathan, the son of Saul, had come to David, he fell on his face and prostrated himself." Then David said, "Mephibosheth?" And he answered, "Here is your servant!" So David said to him, "Do not fear, for I will surely show you kindness for Jonathan, your father's sake and will restore to you all the land of Saul, your grandfather; and ye shall eat bread at my table continually." Then he bowed himself, and said, "What is your servant that you should look upon such a dead dog as I" (2 Samuel 9:1-8).*

This is a day that Mephibosheth should never forget because the favor of God was about to prove itself bigger than the circumstances of life. The mercy of God is about to overcome the attacks of this world. Mercy was apparent all the way down in LoDebar and it was impossible not to see. Word quickly spread through the countryside that "King Saul and Prince Jonathan are dead and David is now King." However, there was no celebration over David's ascension to the throne in the house of Saul. Rather the news brought grief and panic to it, because in those days, it was customary that any king taking the throne would often find it necessary to eliminate the family of the king before him to war against insurrection.

Oblivious to all that was happening, little Mephibosheth was sitting on the floor his nurse bursts in the room, grabs him up, and heads toward the door to safety. In the midst of all the confusion and her haste, she dropped him, crushing his ankles and inevitably crippling him for life.

Understand that Mephibosheth had royal blood flowing through his veins. He was the grandson of Saul, the king of Israel, and the son of Jonathan. He was born into regal splendor in the palace. This meant that he had everything that a little boy could need; the best clothing, the best toys, and the best food. He never lacked for anything while living in the palace. And oh, what a future he had! I would imagine that the family talked about Mephibosheth when he was born—what a beautiful child he was, and how one day he would become a great king. His future was laid out and no one would know what would later happen to him but God.

The palace would only be a memory. The crown would never be placed upon his head. The throne that was planned for him to occupy faded at the death of Saul and Jonathan. As the nurse ran with him clutched in her arms... screams all around her... she trips, and Mephibosheth falls from her arms. He was entrusted into the care of an unnamed nurse, and in a time of haste, he was consequently dropped. He was dropped by the one who fed him; one who hugged him; one who at times placed loving arms around him; one who sung lullabies to him at bedtime. He was dropped by the one that he trusted and loved. Have you ever been dropped by someone you loved and trusted? Have you ever been left high and dry; alone and distressed? As a result of being dropped, you were damaged from that point forward and you began to walk differently. I can see evidence of people having been dropped by their actions. Even their current relationships suffer the effects of them having been dropped. They carry their insecurities which have left them with low self-esteem, a lack of trust and a poor reflection of their own value.

Understand that the Bible constantly affirms the teaching of self -worth. Psalm 8:5 says, *"For thou has made him a little lower than the angels, and has crowned him with glory and honour. Thou madest him to have dominion over the works of thy hands; thou hast put all things under his feet."* We begin to fall into new traps of disappointment because we start justifying other people based on our past experiences. We begin to become disgruntled and develop feelings of hatred. When we fall into the cycle of hating those that have dropped us, we forfeit our right to go on by refusing to forgive. Matthew 5:43-44 says, *"Ye have heard that it hath been said, thou shall love thy neighbor and hate thine enemy. But I say unto you, Love your enemies, bless them that curse you, and do good to them that hate you, and pray for them which despitefully use you, and persecute you..."*

The easiest way to fall into a trap of social disconnect is to dwell on the hurt. Instead of admitting the hurt, we think about it and ponder anger. Anger then becomes so strong that you can never forget that you have been hurt, much less forget who has hurt you. You begin to plot revenge and always find yourself dwelling on the issue. These types of actions will cause your spiritual and natural growth to become stagnate. The mind is now manipulated by your feelings and the initial hurt evolves into something larger than you can hold.

In our fallen world, evil is a painful reality. Every person alive experiences pain. God, however, allows evil to touch our lives for reasons that we cannot understand. We all experience some type of disabling lameness that seems to set our lives on an undesirable course. In life, we are prone to experience all manner of distress. There are natural wrongs such as birth defects, diseases, and tragedies that cannot be traced to any human course (hurricanes, volcanoes, and floods). Although insurance companies may describe the latter as "Acts of God," they are in fact examples of events that strike both the just and the unjust without differentiation. Next, there are inadvertent wrongs; accidents and all other unintentional injuries or damages, for which it is unreasonable to blame anyone. Finally, there are self-inflicted wrongs: misuse of drugs, alcohol, food, or anything else that damages a person's mind, body, or emotions. This category also includes the failure to stay out of dangerous relationships and situations. When something bad happens, we have three choices. We can pretend that it didn't happen (which is to abdicate responsibility), we can host a pity party for ourselves (but the guest will eventually get bored and go on to someone with a more tragic story), or we can acknowledge God's right to allow whatever circumstances into our lives that make us the most useful to Him.

Unwelcomed problems can stimulate spiritual growth. They show us where changes are needed in our character and they deepen our understanding when we seek biblical solutions to them. Problems force us to pray when nothing else seems to be helping. They cleanse our hearts from within and increase our compassion for others.

The Psalmist stated in Psalm119:71, *"It is good for me that I have been afflicted; that I might learn thy statutes."* Nothing makes me know God like the rise of trouble and affliction. We can be moving along with our comfortable lives and all of a sudden God will allow us to experience a crippling situation that results in our being lame. Generally, we find a new dimension in God that we did not know existed, until we are faced with certain situations.

In Samuel 9:8, Mephibosheth referred to himself as a dead dog. This gives us good indications of his state while in Lodebar; one of hopelessness and inactivity. Many people live in a state of loneliness. There are many others who live right in the middle of life's hustle and bustle that find themselves misunderstood and alone. Both physically and psychologically, people have been and are still surrounded by thousands. From the homeless to the struggling single mother, people feel that they are alone. Distressed, depressed, forgotten, and neglected... they feel alone!

Lodebar was a place of loneliness. In fact, it means "not having" or "pasture less." It was a town filled with forgotten people, including Mephibosheth. In Lodebar, one could find the lost, unskilled, and uneducated outcasts of society; those whom people would scorn; those that we pass by and overlook; those who would be considered just another statistic on a government report; those who would be considered as candidates for some PhD. dissertation study.

Lodebar was full of estranged, poverty stricken people with no family or jobs that were barely getting by day to day. Today Lodebar would be filled with distraught people, all with a story, broken pasts, drug addictions, emotional struggles, and psychological traumas. These inhabitants are not all there by their own choice. Mephibosheth was not in Lodebar because of himself, or because of something he had done. He was not born crippled. It was not his fault that his father died. It was not his fault that the nurse dropped him. Nor was it his fault that there were no doctors who could correct his situation.

It may not be your fault that you have been damaged in life. It is not your fault that you were molested as a child. It is not your fault that you were physically or verbally abused; left parentless and having to raise yourself or to raise your parents instead of them raising you. It is not your fault that you were raised in poverty, was a recipient of welfare and handouts; that no one ever gave you guidance, provided you with a good education; inspired you, poured life into you; or built up some confidence in you. It is not your fault! It is not your fault that they closed the business down where you worked. It is not your fault that you have lived or now live in Lodebar.

We are always quickly to assume that people who are in situations worse than our own, have done something wrong to get that way! I have heard preachers say that not only do these people lack faith to change their situations, but they are also being punished by God because they have sinned. Please! These individuals have experienced unexpected turmoil that had left them believing that there was no way out and no one to help. Lodebar was their only choice. It was a place where they could wallow in their situations; a place to share in everyone else's pain, where they would not be judged and a place that no one wanted to bring them out. Nobody wants to go to the ghetto, unless maybe it's to buy some drugs. Nobody wants to go to the homeless shelter, unless it's to receive credit and praise for doing their "part." Nobody wants to go out to poverty stricken country areas, unless it's to buy some vegetables on the side of the road. Nobody comes to Lodebar by choice!

Experiencing Lodebar is like seeing that person who asks you how you are doing, and when you begin to tell them about your troubles, they tune you out and walk away! They are not concerned about how you feel or what you are going through. Most people just don't care. But Jesus said, *"Come unto me, all ye that labor and are heavy laden, and I will give you rest. Take my yoke upon you, and learn of me; for I am meek and lowly in heart: and ye shall find rest unto your souls. For my yoke is easy, and my burden is light."* Only Jesus can rescue someone down in Lodebar.

It is sad to see the number of people who have decided to settle in Lodebar, and have become comfortable in the place where they are originally brought against their will. Lodebar is not only a place for the poor, but it is not always a physical place. There are so many people who are in a state of isolation, brokenness, and confusion because they have been "dropped" by people and situations. More people are dying on the inside, though they appear to have it all together to the average person. Someone very close to you may be crippled today by something that keeps them miserable, unhappy, frustrated, angry, moody, or jealous. They are dealing with something that has caused them to live in a psychological prison where there seems to be no way of escape! They cannot talk to you about it because they are ashamed, worried, embarrassed, or afraid that you may not understand and would probably talk about them.

Church people like to put each other down, as if everybody in the church is perfect. Whereas the church is supposed to be a hospital where people come to get fixed up, not beat up. The truth is, the church is made up of a strange cast of characters and people with all kinds of issues in their past that they have crippled by. Some of us struggle to sleep, and others depend on drugs like Paxel and Ritalin to keep us at ease. The church is full of people in Lodebar. Paul said, *"But God chose the foolish things of the world to shame the wise; God chose the weak things of the world to shame the strong."* It is because of Him that you are in Christ Jesus, who has become for us wisdom from God, that is, our righteousness, holiness and redemption. Therefore, as it is written: 'Let him who boasts boast in the Lord.'"

People are afraid to come out of Lodebar and ask for help. They are worried that they will be put down, talked about, and insulted. Fear, more than anything else, keeps us down. Isn't it strange the things that we fear in life? We fear rejection, failure, and other people, but we do not fear God. Even though Jesus said, *"Do not be afraid of those who kill the body but cannot kill the soul. Rather, be afraid of the one who can destroy both the soul and body in hell."*

It is time that we discover what has us bound to Lodebar; this state of depression, fear, loneliness, sadness, and shame. We have to decide that there is a place in the palace for me, where I can be honored, understood, loved, and treated as royalty. You are royalty and there was no royal court in Lodebar—come out.

Saved But Miserable 11

I knew that living for God would be much better than the life I lived before I knew God. However, I was under the impression that coming into the knowledge and power of God would free me from entanglements of the world. I came into the church with the understanding that I would live a life of peace, holiness and righteousness from that point onward. After all, God had proven Himself to me in so many ways that surely He was going to do this. However, those who told me about the peace didn't make the timeframe clear for "my peace." I had to later learn that the peace of God and learning to live a life of holiness was a process. The righteousness of God was not due to my lifestyle, but His goodness. Nonetheless, the church was filled with people whose counsel was that after receiving Christ, everything in my life would be solved and I should never worry or sin again. All of their counsel made serving Jesus such a chore. Instead of helping me, it left me frustrated, confused and brought an unbearable level of guilt.

Jesus said, *"I came that they may have life, and that they might have it more abundantly"* (John 10:10). I knew that something very wonderful happened to me when I accepted the salvation of Christ. There were immediate and obvious changes that happened in my life as a result of the teachings and guidance that I received from those in the church. Partly from those who fed the word of God to me as a young child. Those were the seeds that were deposited deep inside of me and eventually germinated into the reality of knowing that Jesus does save. Those seeds taught me that I did not deserve salvation and because of great grace it was offered to me anyway. I am so thankful that I responded to the offer of salvation through faith and without question. Those were the days of my infancy and innocence, before I learned how to complain and ask questions. This was before my ideals were shattered and the reality that everybody who ascended to salvation didn't live a life without sin. Some even wrestled with continual and frequent sin. Imagine my horror to find that part of that struggle was also in me.

I can remember feeling so condemned after every service. I thought that I must not love God like I should or that something was wrong with me. I thought, "Why am I still lying and why is my mind still thinking such thoughts." I made the assumption that the rest of the congregation had overcome in these areas. Because of the sin that I knew that was in my life, I often felt out of place and did not feel like I was worthy to participate in worship service. Hearing so many indictments of my life eventually gave way to God revealing to me the inconsistencies in others' lives, and sometimes in the lives of those who condemned me. I eventually came to the conclusion that I knew from the start, that all have sinned and fallen short of the glory of God. Sin is what we needed Jesus to take away from us; faith is all we could bring to him. Instead of examining myself, I had to reexamine the word that said that we are saved by grace through faith (Ephesians 2:8). I no longer had to be miserable; cheerless; joyless, full of grim, depressed, downhearted, low-spirited, despondent, and sad. I did not think that being saved should make you feel that way. I did not have a desire to commit sin. I just wanted to live. At one point, I remember thinking, "There has to be more to serving God than where you go, what you do, who you see, what you wear, and how you speak." God had to have had a greater purpose for us. The frustration of just coming to church, but never really knowing the God of the church made me miserable. How was I ever going to deal with the damages of my life, if I spent all of my time dealing with the requirements of the church?

I was miserable—saved but miserable. So miserable that the same services that I used to eagerly await, became a burden to attend. I dreaded coming because I feared being reminded of my inconsistent lifestyle and my ultimate trip to hell, according to them. I was miserable. I began to feel that I no longer loved God, nor was I loved by God because of these sins that still operated in my life and my thoughts. I became conscious and guilty of every sin and I mean every sin. At one point, I can remember feeling so guilty that I asked the pastor if I could meet with him because something was bothering me. He agreed and when I came into his office I started telling him that I had backslidden from the faith and needed to be restored. I could tell that he was a little taken back by this because I was a young believer, but I was very active in our church and extremely faithful to the mission of the church, in attendance, outreach and service. He proceeded to ask me what I had done and I can remember telling him that I was a little embarrassed but I shared with him that I had been struggling with masturbating. Today I can still remember the look on his face and how I felt when I was sitting in that office. I said I have been struggling with it before and since I have given my life to Christ. I went on to say that I needed him to pray with me so that God would set me free me of this sin. His response to me was surprising, because I thought that he would ask me to sit out of active participation in our services, inform the congregation that I was a sinner and to stay away from me until I got the victory over my life. He didn't do any of that. What he did was shared with me that I was about to enter into a long journey of learning how to please God and my part of this adventure was to keep a desire to please Him and His part was to give me power to please Him. He went on to say that there would be times when I would fail, but respond to it as I had done in the past, understanding that I had missed the mark but to continue to press for that mark. When he finished speaking I was left with those words, go back and continue to "press for that mark." I cannot tell you how liberating those words were for me. It helped me understand that I had not reached the mark but I am pressing for it. In fact, none of us have reached the mark, but we are only pressing toward it. I had been living my life to reach the mark that people had set which proved to be too grievous.

I had lost the real goal as it relates to my faith, which was the prize of the high calling of God in Christ Jesus. My life had become religiously regimented and stale. It had reached a placed where I no longer enjoyed my faith. Where was the joy of walking with God? The continued expectancies of man, which were not of God, drove me to dread the life that I once embraced.

While driving frequently over the last ten years, I had never been cited for violating the traffic laws. However, in the last few weeks I have been cited twice for highway violations. Since I do not want another ticket, I have slowed down and I adhere to the posted speed limits. Since that time, I noticed that all of the cars and trucks ahead of me soon disappeared from sight. But behind me, they began to pile up. Right on my bumper was an eighteen-wheeler truck, and another one was directly behind it! Within seconds, I knew that it was either break the posted speed limit and drive 70, or get run over by an angry truck driver! With no place I could, and nothing else I could do, I put my foot on the gas and rushed through the 11 mile long construction zone under great duress.

We live in a complex world that rushes madly onward. You are expected to either, "push, pull, or get out of the way." There are times when we feel that we are about to be "run over" because we simply can't keep up with man's demands on our lives. Many of us are "worn out physically;

and burned out spiritually." We have come to the end of our rope and there doesn't seem to be enough rope left to tie a knot so that we might hang on! This is how I felt in those early days of my Christian journey. I felt like I was being forced to speed my way to perfection and get to where I was going in a record time. I became very stressed and bitter. There is a passage of scripture in Matthew 6:34, where we find Jesus offering sound advice to men and women who were very much like modern man today. Men and women who had hopes and dreams that were often shattered by the realities of life. They too suffered from worries and frustrations that had piled up on them, leaving them not knowing exactly how to cope. Jesus' advice to them was simply this: "Don't borrow trouble from tomorrow. Don't be anxious about it, or even give thought to it."

Some wise person coined the phrase "What you don't know can't hurt you." I suppose that in part that statement is true because what you don't know simply cannot play on your mind. We often talk about the fact that we are engaged in spiritual warfare, and the battlefield is the mind. One might say that the pressures I felt from others, was a result of how I was thinking. Nevertheless, the pressure was real for me.

Satan fights against us by filling our minds with negative thoughts that create worries and frustrations that cause our minds to spin out of control. All too often, our concentration or focus is misdirected. We tend to focus on the negative thoughts because we want to stand in readiness against that which threatens us. As we think negative thoughts, we become more and more overwhelmed, instead of finding relief through solutions.

Weighed by the balance of our mind, whatever we focus on becomes greater in power and influence. Let me suggest that much of the unhappiness in the church does not come from what others expect of you, but what you think about yourself. Your emphasis on their expectations can either add or relieve your stress. In his letter to the believers at Philippi, Apostle Paul exhorted them (Philippians 4:8) saying: *"...whatsoever things are just; whatsoever things are pure; whatsoever things are lovely; whatsoever things are of good report; if there be any virtue, and if there be any praise, thing on these things."* A paraphrase of Paul's exhortation might be something like this: If there is any intrinsic character-building value or anything note-worthy and commendable in something let such fill your mind.

So much of what we give our attention to is negative and destructive. We tend to have thoughts that draw us away from the things that are essential in our lives because someone or something comes along and discolors how we see them. So, the real key is to change our thought process and not to allow the pressures of what others expect of you cloud your mind so that you can't continue to enjoy what God is doing in you. Deliberately change your focus! Rather than seeing ourselves as powerless, we must visualize ourselves as powerful. You must recognize that our power is not in nor of ourselves, but in God, and in His word. Paul wrote in his letter to the Corinthians, *"for though we walk in the flesh, we do not war after the flesh: (For the weapons of our warfare are not carnal, but mighty through God to the pulling down of strongholds); casting down imaginations, and every high thing that exalteth against the knowledge of God, and bringing into captivity every thought to the obedience of Christ..."* (2 Corinthians 10:3-5).

It is certain that there are many circumstances and situations in our life that we cannot change. They are beyond our control and power. Therefore, we are faced with a choice: We can either accept them or we allow them to drive us to distraction through worry and frustration. In some cases, we find out what God is requiring of us. There is a clear oppression that's deposited on us by their rules as we enter into the Christian life.

Today, so many believers feel trapped and stressed by what they perceive to be the dichotomy of living a life where they always feel like they have fallen short. Aren't you tired of being miserable? After King David sinned against God and slept with Bathsheba, he had her husband Uriah sent into the heat of battle to ensure that he would be killed. When he thought he had gotten away with it, God sent Nathan to remind him that this was not hidden from Him. The reason some of us will never know what God wants from us is because we are overly concerned with how we are perceived by man, and we do not have enough concern with how we are seen by God. One reason for our frustration and why we find ourselves so miserable is because we have not been honest before God.

David said in Psalms 51:10, *"Create in me a clean heart, O God, and renew a right spirit within me."* The scripture suggests that David was in need of restoration from God. By his own admission, he needed his spirit renewed. Anytime something has expired, such as a credit card, it must be renewed. When your license plate on your car expires, you can no longer legally drive your car. The license plate has to be renewed. After so many years of being in church, something happens to us that most of us do not realize. In order to continue to live as a Christian, your spirit must be renewed. If you are going to please and serve God, there must continual seasons when your spirit is renewed. The Psalmist writes further in verse twelve, *"Restore unto me the joy of thy salvation."* If you are miserable, this should be a clear sign that you need your joy restored.

Another reason why we are so miserable in faith is because we are waiting. Anyone who has committed to serving God understands that there will be times when you have to wait on God. Too often, we can't handle God's delays. As much as we trust God now and believe that our circumstances will eventually change, we struggle with understanding delays. There are literally volumes of thematic discussions in the Old Testament dealing with the issue of delay. The historiography of the children of Israel is foremost among them in helping us to understand our promise. Hearing a promise can be a long way from actually obtaining the promise. Our faith accepts the word that God speaks, but we must also accept the fact that the same word we so eagerly received may be hidden and hindered for years before it manifests.

God said that He would open the door but you have

literally gone through hell, pitfalls, and episodes in your life that were trying to keep the door shut. What we have to learn is that shut doors cannot stop you from going in when God has made you a promise. Bad news only forces you to remember that the spoken word is not dependent on you, but it has to be fulfilled when God says so—in His time. This is exactly what we see in this text. God tells Moses to go before Pharaoh because it is time to let the people go. But the moment Moses spoke it Pharaoh started shutting the door. Instead of changing his heart, the Bible says that God hardened his heart. *"Who is the Lord that I should obey His voice to let Israel go? The people of the land are many and you want them to rest from their labors: But I commanded now to no longer give them straw to make brick and the tally of the brick should not diminish any."* I do not understand why there is a fire started whenever God says anything about our life. However, I do know that we have to first be tested before we can be trusted, and we have to be able to wait for the spoken promise by God; even when it doesn't appear to be coming.

Do you remember when Elijah was on Mt. Carmel? Before he could ask for the fire to fall, God told him to make it harder by telling the men to put water in the trenches. Before Gideon went down to fight against the enemy, God took all his help and left him with only three hundred men. Before Samson began to experience deliverance, he had to be blinded, deceived, and taken captive by his foes. I don't know why God uses exaggerated circumstances as catalysts to our victory, but He wants to make it clear that without Him you will never come out of your situation. Your ability to trust Him when something is delayed is a real sign of your trust. That's why He makes us the underdogs, the outnumbered, and the least likely, before He opens the doors and gives us the land.

You Have Got To Be Desperate   12

B eing "damaged" in life is going to happen. If you could understand that those places where you have been broken and damaged are the best places for you to seek help from God. *"And He said unto me, My grace is sufficient for thee: for my strength is made perfect in weakness. Mostly gladly therefore will I rather glory in my infirmities, that the power of Christ may rest upon me"* (2 Corinthians 12:9). Who knows, maybe without them we would remain self-sufficient, complacent and void of the presence of God? There is nothing like trouble to wake us up and help us understand what it takes to get something from the Lord. In 1 Samuel Chapter 1, we are introduced to a woman who was desperate for a child and because of the custom of her time; she was ridiculed for what she could do nothing about. We are not told how often or how insensitive her mockers were but coupled with her own pressure of not being able to have children and the stigma by others, she must have been damaged. This woman was Hannah; she was one of the most gracious women in the entire Bible. As a matter of fact, the name Hannah means *gracious* or to look favorable upon. So, when her parents named her Hannah, they were actually calling her favored. This is a word from heaven for somebody who is reading this; you can be favored and not appear to be favored.

Even in her barrenness, her husband Elkanah loved her. He even went so far as to show favoritism to Hannah by giving her twice as much as he gave his other wife. He worked very hard to make sure that Hannah was secure in their relationship. He loved, cared and provided for her. However, the problem with Elkanah was, he could never be enough to repair the brokenness of not having a child. I find this to be very interesting that people spend a great deal of time masking and substituting things that they get in life for what they really want in life. They do this in hope of avoiding the broken and empty places in their life. Many people hope to satisfy themselves with replacements to what they really desire for themselves. Elkanah thought he could give Hannah enough to replace what she really longed for; he could never become what she longed to have.

Hannah was damaged and at the center of her life stood her barrenness. Her husband asks, "Hannah, why do you weep and why do you not eat; and why does your heart grieve. Am I not better than even ten sons?" Elkanah tried very hard to understand her but that would never be enough to please her. If barrenness were not enough, Hannah felt the wretchedness of sharing a love that should have been all her own. Finally, to add insult to injury, the woman that she shared her husband with was so jealous of the way that Elkanah blessed her that she reminded Hannah daily of her barrenness. I call this the spirit of Peninnah or the spirit of jealousy. The problem is it is not limited to Old

Testament characters, but is often found on many church pews, where instead of relating to the pain of someone else, you are only concerned with them not being as wanted as you.

The Bible said that Hannah was a woman of sorrowful spirit. The positive side to that is that sorrows are seeds from whence songs evolve. There is no real song without experiencing real sorrow. One might be a good singer, but when someone breaks your heart, you evolve into a great one. Some things cannot be taught—we just have to go through some real trouble in life to know them. You can never be able to successfully teach prosperity until you have come through poverty. When God brings you out of poverty, there is a sense of deep appreciation in your spirit and you will find yourself thanking God for things that other people think are normal. Victory is relative to struggle and what one person may get easy, another can only gain through years of toiling. Your praise is also relative to your struggle. Whenever you see a person so consumed with praise in a church service, do not always assume that some wonderful thing has happened in their lives and they are not familiar with the struggles of your own. To the contrary, exaggerated praise can often be a result of what has not happened in their lives and their level expectation. There are times it is a result of their deep appreciation for God allowing them to make it to another day. Sometimes your place of poverty brings out your best praise.

Hannah had favor, but her barrenness was a type of poverty. Seeds of greatness and favor are rarely recognizable through conditions. Some of us are holding seeds of favor in our life but won't recognize them until they have been processed through struggle over time. Those very things that make you cry will cause you to rejoice later. *"He that goeth forth weeping, bearing precious seeds with him will doubtless come again rejoicing."* Your words are seeds and the Bible clearly states that "by the foolishness of preaching men are delivered." Preaching will plant a seed in your spirit that will cause you to shake yourself. It will wake up something in you that has been asleep or lying dormant that you thought would never live again. Because of the power of words, we have to be careful who we allow to preach, encourage, or speak to us. Their words can confuse us as well as tamper with our faith. They may alter our destiny, they may cause us to abort our purpose, or they may even set us back. Their words may cause us to bring forth fruit of low self-esteem, discouragement, depression and sin.

Hannah had favor but she also had grief. She received what the Bible refers to as a "worthy portion," which means that she received what she needed and some extra stuff. I don't know how many times God just gave me extra stuff. What I call extra stuff is the stuff that no one but God could give me and things that were beyond what was necessary to sustain me. God gave me exceeding, abundantly, above all that I could ask or think. These types of "extra" blessings are often the blessings that define my praise. Many people are suspicious of people who are exaggerated in their praise to God and see it as emotionalism and unnecessary. It may be unnecessary to some, but it is warranted. It is not always a result of emotionalism, but gratitude.

Hannah was blessed but the barrenness in her body was producing bitterness in her spirit. She could have done like Sarah and told her husband to put the woman out. She could have retaliated and lost her dignity, but she decided to pray. In fact, it was living with her persecutor Peninnah, that that forced her to pray.

The name Peninnah in Hebrews mean "rounded like a pearl." Pearls are beautiful and women love them, but remember pearls are created out of agitation. They are created by a grain of sand easing its way down into a clam or an oyster. Calcium deposits begin to develop and wrap themselves around that grain of sand. Out of that irritation emerges a pearl. There is something about irritation that takes you to the next level. Peninnah's name actually means irritation and believe it or not, there are some things that God will allow into your life just to irritate you.

Some people were sent into your life by God with the assignment of irritation. Everyone is not in your life because they love and believe in you or necessarily want to help you. Every now and then God will allow a little "grain of sand" to get to you. People act as though those grains of sand sent into their lives are needless interruptions, but I have found that even though they frustrate you; they will eventually evolve into something precious. We do not like to talk about or be confronted by the Peninnah's of life. But without them irritating us, we will never seek God for those things that are missing in our life. Only irritation, dissatisfaction, discontentment and need will usher us into seeking God.

Seeking after God is not a natural thing. It usually takes some situation or something to usher us into pursuit of God's plan. Situations like life-threatening diseases, pink slips, bad marriages, or runaway children are the types of conditions that make us cry out in prayer to God. We do not like to seek God because seeking is frustrating and it laborious. It's almost like losing your keys: frustrating and irritating. You do not look for your keys until you are ready to go somewhere. When you realize that you have a situation that requires seeking God, meaning that you are in desperate need, then you do so with focus, passion, and an extreme since of seriousness. Wanting what we do not have always makes us try that much harder to get it. It is probably easier to be comfortable and satisfied with what you already have, but who wants to remain almost whole, almost blessed, almost favored, and almost successful? There are some people who have come too close to success and will literally spend the rest of their lives "almost" there. Even if it costs us what we already have, we should make the decision to go after what we have not gained.

What Hannah was saying was there is something missing. There is another story in the Bible about a woman who lost a coin. It must have been valuable to her because she apparently discontinued the routine of her day and made finding the coin the priority of her day. She moved the furniture and swept the floor until she found it. Many of us have been sweeping life's floors looking for what has been missing. We sweep through one church to another church, from one relationship to another relationship, from one club into another club, or from one bed into another bed, trying to find what has been missing. Hannah had a nice life, a nice husband and a good reputation. But she was desperate to have the thing that was missing—a child. Many stores have special sections for items that are considered to be damaged goods. These items either have been scratched or dented that has caused them to be labeled as "DAMAGED." Because of this new label, the value of these items has been decreased and more than likely will continue to decrease in value until somebody takes them off the shelf. In some cases, these items though marked down still don't sell and will eventually be discarded. The stores position is that the damage that the item sustained rendered it of no value to the customer; therefore it has no value to them. Only an all-powerful, almighty God could issue a new label to something that has been damaged, broken, or torn and increase its value to make it "priceless." This is exactly what happens when we receive God's stamp of deliverance.

We read in 1 Samuel, chapter 1 that Hannah prayed to God in verse 11 *"Then she made a vow and said, "O Lord of hosts, if You will indeed look on the affliction of Your maidservant and remember me, and not forget Your maidservant, but will give your maidservant a child, then will I give him to the Lord all the days of his life, and no razor shall come upon his head."* The priest Eli thought Hannah was drunk, but Hannah let him know otherwise. Her reply to Eli's false accusation was, "I am a woman of sorrowful spirit. I have drunk neither wine nor intoxicating drink, but have poured out my soul before the Lord. Do not consider your maidservant a wicked woman, for out of the abundance of my complaint and grief I have spoken until now." She was not drunk, she was just desperate. When you are barren in your life and intent on breaking that spirit of oppression and hopelessness over your soul the only place to go is to God.

It amazes me how God can take a hopeless situation and turn it into a time of great rejoicing. One word from God can change your whole outlook on life. Hannah eventually conceived and gave birth to a son whom she called Samuel. She remained faithful in her vow to the Lord and was so grateful for all that the Lord had done for her. She was no longer barren, but fruitful. She was no longer a sorrowful woman, but a woman filled with great joy. The Lord has a way of silencing our accusers. He has a way of bringing His people through difficult circumstances and brokenness. He requires that we "get desperate" and pursue Him even when it looks like you can't hold on.

If we would be honest, all of us can say that there are areas in our lives that are damaged and times that we thought we could have given up. However, there are some believers who refuse to live without or beneath what God has already spoken for their lives. You must become desperate if you desire God to change the situation and help you destroy the stronghold. When we find ourselves broken instead of desperate, we learn to mask the scars of our past experiences to fit quietly within the perfect mold of those around us. We learn to become social chameleons, puppets, and religious pretenders who pretend to be somewhere we are not.

It is never best to mask your scars and pretend that your dilemmas do not have purpose. We do God an injustice when we camouflage what is happening in our lives, and put them on our list of untouchable subjects. We must have a high opinion of ourselves if we think we can pull off the masquerade of presenting ourselves without weaknesses, failures, hang-ups and sin. God is not surprised by our lives in any way. He understands our frame and knows the numbers of hairs on our head. God knows how He designed you for every struggle and every pain. We would be better off if we could admit our nakedness before men, because it is clear that we are already naked before God.

Moses spent a great deal of discussion in Exodus 4, arguing his limitations as if God was not aware of them. I believe that part of the reason why so many of us hide our scars, failures, and limitations is because we think that people are not aware of them. There is something in us that makes us want to be seen as capable, even in places where we are not capable. We are threatened by our damaged places that have left us vulnerable, so we think that if we let them show somebody will take advantage of us. However, we have all had situations that left us damaged and even though we are past them, we cannot be surprised when our scars point back to those damaged places.

Live With the Scars

The thing that I have learned is that we are not aware of our capacity to handle conflict and pain. We have a greater threshold than we know, and a larger ability to recover, than we could imagine. We are frightened by what we face, and afraid of the consequences of our decisions. However, if we could reflect back over our lives, we would see that we made it out of storms quickly. Many times we never even look back to remember that we did not think we would survive. How many times have you thought, "This time I'm really in trouble," but you get out tomorrow with hardly even a scratch?

Every now and then we run upon what I call a "defining moment," that pulls us out of our average day and establishes a mark on our lives so great that it leaves us changed. A circumstance or decision so remarkable that it challenges even our faith and we ask, "What am I going to do next? Not your average run-of-the- mill occurrence, but a real snapshot of some point in your life when you have to decide something that will permanently change your life. That is where I was when I came to my destiny and tried to cope with the many situations that left me scarred and damaged. I had to come to a state in life where I decided that in order for me to continue to live in comfort I would have to surrender to what I believed God was leading and pushing me to. It should have been difficult, because this decision could not be made without cost. Every time you come to this place of decision in your life you can expect it to be agonizing because you cannot just consider where you are going, but there must be some reflection back to where you have already been.

My deciding to accept my brokenness and my past

without shame, as a part of God's plan, meant that I would have to expose my broken areas to people who had never seen them before. These people could see me differently, threatening my status and position. I ran the risk of being considered unsaved or not loving God as I should, because of those areas that were not totally surrendered to God. This was a defining moment for me because I concluded that God had created some high-minded purpose in all of my experiences. There must be a purpose in all of my scars.

We all have scars. Sometimes we are scarred by others, situations, or by our own choices. David failed God horribly by taking the wife of Uriah for himself. He was a giant slayer and a man after God's own heart; the one who God made an everlasting covenant, and inarguably the greatest King of Israel. David could master a lot of things, but he could not master the entrants of his flesh. He was found to be a man of passions, saddled with the propensity to sin. Though he knew God, he didn't always glorify God. The Bible said that God had to send Nathan to remind him that He knew him better than he knew himself. God said, *"I have anointed you King over Israel and I delivered you from the hand of Saul. I gave your master's house to you, and your master's wives into your arms. I gave you the house of Israel and Judah. And if all this had been too little, I would have given you even more"* (II Samuel 12:8).

I often wonder if the charades that we play with each other offend God. The problem with hiding things about your life is—you get good at it, which means you will always do it. David was obviously committed to his game and good at it. He thought that if one thing went wrong with one of his moves, he would proceed with Plan B and then Plan C, and so on. He did this until finally, it cost Uriah his life. What David did not realize is that the people were not the ones who neither held him up, nor was his reputation because of people, it was because of God. David knew what was expected of him by God and by the people. But he was not ready to live up to it. Instead of crying to God for help, he continued to hide his sin. He remembered that he was a king. He continued to try to make the situation go away when he really should have tried to face it. If you have ever been wounded, left with scars, or tried to fix something that you messed up, then you know that it will soon get out of hand. There are generally no shortcuts, or any easy answers. You just have to face, right away.

Not all wounds are self-inflicted. If you continue to live, you will soon learn that there will always be situations and people who will leave you scarred. You are going to be afflicted, and whether you serve God or not, there will be some trouble that you will not be able to avoid. Some things will be significant, and even after you are healed, you will have to deal with the memories of the pain. There will be times when it is difficult to forgive others for what they have done to you. What you have to understand is that there are reasons why you have faced these trials.

When I look at the places of my wounds, I see the many times I should have been derailed or left for dead. I have even asked why God He would continue to use me. The more I look at the scars, the more I begin to understand something about my scars. Every time my mind reflects back to one of the situations that left the wound, I'm reminded of how wonderful God has been. God did not give me into my enemy's hands. I remember that He is God. People who tried to hurt me were not able to destroy me because they are not God. Always remember that God is in control. Your life or your success is not finished unless God says, "It is done." If God be for you, who can be against you?

In 2 Corinthians 12:7-9, Paul departs from his usual focus of defending the faith, because he found it necessary to defend himself against the challengers of his faith. The truth is, no matter how incredibly anointed you may be, something or somebody will be sent into your life to challenge your faith. You may be living in a painful part of your life currently. Just remember that some things are necessary and you may never have the chance to prove your testimony unless some things are sent into your life. No test, no testimony.

Some things that we will face may make it feel hard for us to do the work of God. It can be a person, situation, or illness, but it has been designed to make the work of God difficult for us. Usually, this happens when we have become determined to do more for God in spite of our circumstances. All of a sudden, you begin to deal with inconvenient circumstances and unexplainable storms. The messengers of Satan had been sent to buffet you, stop you from completing your assignment and challenge your faith.

People always sound so anointed when they talk about being faithful when things go wrong. Understand that they weren't necessarily sounding like this while they were going through their storm. It is easy to talk about rebuking the devil and ignoring trouble when there is not a thorn pricking you in your side. Wait until everything in your life is disrupted and out of place, and you become confused about what God is doing. Wait until you start asking for relief from God and there are no signs of help or relief on the way. Everybody has a sunshine praise when everything is going right in life, but what happens to that praise when the messenger of Satan is sent to conjure up a real storm. What are you going to do when it looks like your religion is not adding anything to your life, you are unemployed, your bills are behind, you don't have any money, and you can't even answer your phone because you know it's a bill collector? Will you still be able to praise God? I used to think that I could never be sad and it never entered my mind to give up because I thought, "I'm too anointed to fail." I now know that a big storm in your life can cause you to rethink everything you thought that you knew. You can be so hurt, disappointed, and broken that while everyone around you is praising God, you just sit in your seat because you are trying to understand what is going on. We think we can handle anything, but as soon as we feel the pain of being lied on and having our name dragged through the mud, we learn otherwise.

It is necessary that God allow us to have some troubles in our lives to prepare us for the real struggles that are to come. The contest in which Paul writes to the Corinthians was to vindicate the purity of his life and the authority of his ministry, against those who would say that he should not be an apostle. His challenge now was not with those who did not believe in God, but with those who claimed to know Him. Many of the thorns that God allows to be sent to you will come from inside your circle and will be the most effective ones. I have learned that the reason they are more effective is because they pack the biggest surprise. It is hard to prepare to be hurt by people you love. There is a certain level that you will never get to until God allows something to come into your life to strip you, so that He can use you; without pride, self-righteousness, envy, jealousy, deceit, or hate. All of Jacob's life he wrestled with trying to get the attention of God by attempting to fulfill what he and his mother thought he should have. Jacob did not understand the ways of God. He did not understand that he did not have to manipulate the plan. God had to leave him changed and with a limp so that he would know that he could do nothing on his own.

Everybody is not able to handle the kind of anointing and power that is tied to having a revelation from God. I know that I wasn't. God had to break me, strip me, and send some thorns into my life before I was ready to serve Him with humility. God has put this treasure in earthen vessels that the excellence of power may be of Him and not of us. He deposited the rich things of Him in us and that requires that there be some preparation in us. Before He can give us revelation, He gives us afflictions that will threaten our strength but build our trust. Nothing that God tells us will be easy and it will require us to stand and decide. Before I met God, things in my life were not pain free. I just experienced a different kind of trouble. Paul was faithful to God, yet his life was full of turmoil, and conflict.

Paul said, "Of the Jews five times received I forty stripes saved one. Three times I was beaten with rods, once I was stoned, three times I was shipwrecked. I spent the night and a day in the open sea. I have been constantly on the move. I have been in danger from rivers, in danger from bandits, in danger form my own countrymen, in danger from Gentiles; in danger in the city, in danger in the country, in danger at sea; and in danger from false brothers. And besides everything else, I face daily pressures of my concern for all churches..." This writing by Paul is a word for you. You should expect to experience pressures in the church.

Paul had to defend himself against his critics who did not know the price he had to pay to get where he was. Everyone does not know you, nor do they know the price that you have paid to walk with God. Remember, you have given up so much already to be free in God, so never feel intimidated when you have to give up some people. If they are keeping you from getting to where you are going, then give them up. If they are not walking in the same level of faith that you are trying to create in your life, you must give them up.

I have been given so many revelations from God that He has purposely allowed some things to come into my life, to keep me from being conceited. We do not know what Paul's thorn was; some say it was eye trouble; some thought it to be headaches, epilepsy, or fever, but we know it was so frustrating to him that he kept asking God to take it from him. A thorn is something small in size, like a splinter, which causes a huge irritation. Thorns are those things in our lives that just annoy and distract us. They cause us to think more about the thorn than about serving God. They have become physical burdens pressing against our spirit man and are bothersome.

Do you have anything you are living with that has become bothersome? Maybe it's your job, a person in your life, or perhaps a condition in your body that is bothersome. I trust that God knows how to humble and buffet you, and has created the right weakness in you. Never despise what God is doing in your life, because God said that His strength is made perfect in our weakness.

Leave Me Broken   13

I no longer resent the difficult places and difficult people of my past. I have even come to embrace the damages they were left behind. I no longer hide my failures, scars, weaknesses, and broken places as though they are impediments or hindrances to my victories or marks of shame in my life. I now understand that being dropped in my past has set off a series of complicated, unpredictable, yet wonderful events in me, that have shaped me to become who I am right now. You may not like who you are right now, but let me assure you that your circumstances are working to produce building blocks that will shape your life. They are teaching you to trust God and believe that you cannot be hindered. Even your handicaps help you to see that nothing shall be impossible for you.

Having the ability and strength are things that are advantages in the physical world, but the work of God does not require ability as much as it requires availability. Being available to God is the only necessary element for Him to use you. God has chosen the foolish things of the world to shame the wise, and He has chosen the weak things of the world to shame the things that are strong. Being broken and damaged in a lot of places, means that you are a good candidate for God to choose and use you. All of our flaws, defeats, imperfections, and weaknesses have the power to distract us and hinder our effectiveness in life, but God uses them to push us forward.

The most liberating passage of scripture I have heard was written by Paul to the Romans saying, "... *all things work together for good to them that love God, to them who are called according to his purpose.*" I learned from it that if we are going to believe this text, and I do, that regardless of what happens; we conclude that it is working for our good. You may be struggling with forgiving people who have disappointed you, living with situations that have depressed you, or maybe you are secretly bitter about the way God has afflicted you. Whatever has happened in your life was done for your good. Joseph was put in prison, and though he had been forgotten by the butler, God is always working things together for your good and He is always working in your favor.

In Genesis 50:20, Joseph said these words to his brothers who had come to repent because of the way they treated him all those years. "...ye thought evil against me; but God meant it unto good..." The intent of God will always work in your life despite every work of man. When it looks like your best days are over, God's plans are still at work in your life. Wherever you are at this moment, let me assure you that your situation has a purpose. In Psalm 119,

Delivered But Damaged II

David says, *"It is good for me that I have been afflicted, that I might learn thy statutes."* Have you ever considered how much you have learned through your afflictions and what things the troubles in your life produced? God constantly uses the weak and infirmed people to do great things.

I can still recall the day when I was first saved, and how new I felt, as if I was alive again in so many ways. I can remember thinking that I had been given a new start, a fresh beginning, and that I had permission to begin my life again. In years past, I lived according to my own desires and did not serve God. Now none of that mattered because I could begin again. I felt that nothing could ever distract me, stress me, or depress me because of what I had found in God. What I did not know was that even though I was saved from my past, inside of my mind were still many of the memories of my past. All of these thoughts, memories, and bondages were not eliminated the day that I was saved. I still had many weaknesses, frustrations, and places that I had not forgiven that were still very much with me. I was delivered from sin, but I had been damaged by life and it was those damages that were not allowing me to move forward.

Admitting this and being able to confront it will liberate you like nothing else in the world. You may carry expectations of being superman and imagine that you can go on if those areas do not exist; but they do. You can play church games forever about loving everybody and act as though life is wonderful, and everything is going the way you planned, but until you can be alright with the broken areas in your life only then will God have a chance to perfect you. You may be ridiculed in your circle because of the questions you have about your life and the struggles of your faith, but bringing these issues out into the open will allow somebody to speak into that area of your faith. Remember, we all are facing issues and none of us are immune.

All of us brought something into this faith that did not immediately drop off the moment we accepted Christ. You are not alone in your broken places and in your areas of weakness, or your desire to quit. The church of God is full of people who have testimonies just like yours. We are people who have overcome in some areas of our lives, but have not overcome in others; people who gave up some things years after they should have and held on to some things longer than they needed to. The truth is all of us are going through a process and though we are at different levels in it, it is still the same process. We are all at different levels of knowing God and different places of surrendering to God, but we are all in the process. Don't ever let anyone destroy you in this journey because of where you are in your process. Everybody doesn't understand your brokenness, nor do they know your damages.

I can recall when my son was a small child; he would always have one of my neckties with him. He would keep it near his bed, because my wife and I had begun to wean him from sleeping in our room. For a long time, he and his necktie were inseparable. But we didn't care because it got him out of our room. But eventually the necktie just disappeared and we never saw it again. What happened? When he was in our room, he knew we were there—he had us. However, when we forced him into his own room, he found something to replace our being there. Finally, as he continued to mature, he did not need the necktie, but his dependency shifted to something else. It is through this process of maturity that we learn to depend on God.

We depend on a lot of things until we come to the place where we can depend on Him. That is why God can take the weakest link and call them because when they get to the right place in the process, they will depend on Him. He takes the most disturbing people with the most disturbing stories, and He puts situations in their lives to help them depend on Him.

I've discovered that there are great benefits in being damaged, and having broken places that won't ever be fixed, as Paul's thorn. It is in those places that we cannot depend on ourselves, but we are left with no other choice but to depend on God. It is in those people, who are incapable that God demonstrates to us that He is capable. So, leave me broken the way I am.

We often wish our lives had no imperfect places; no temptations or struggles; anger or jealousy; or vices. When we come to God we often bring all of these things to the table. Moses brought his inability to speak and his murderous past; Esau brought his cunningness; David brought a spirit of lust; and Peter brought a terrible temper. We all bring something that doesn't reflect the very person of Christ, but when we come to Him, we bring all of these things to the table. God does not reject us because of them, but rather creates a testimony through them that will cause men to glorify Him by our victories. So leave me broken just the way I am.

The strength of God is made perfect in my weakness. Paul boasted in his weaknesses and sufferings for Christ; not in his position, achievements, accomplishments, or glories. Men have a tendency to not applaud rejections, weaknesses, sufferings, and shameful experiences. But God uses them powerfully. God could remove these pains from us to give us victory at any time that He desires. Instead of waiting for us to get the victory over our weaknesses, He shows His power in them. Sometimes it is even necessary for God to show us our weaknesses and leave us with areas that are broken.

Paul had experienced the spiritual power of Christ so mightily, that God gave him a thorn in his flesh to ensure that there was no danger that he might begin to think too highly of himself. Paul prayed three times for God to remove the thorn and God refused to remove it. If you have been serving God and faithful to the work of God, and you are seeing areas that will not disappear no matter how much you ask God, then perhaps it is one of those things that God has refused to remove. Maybe he wants to make sure you do not get puffed up or perhaps He wants to reveal His power in you. Maybe God wants to teach you to live for the sake of Christ and not yourself. We do not always know the reason why we are broken, but knowing why you are broken is not the same as accepting where you are broken. If you understand that God can use you broken, it is easier to accept your brokenness.

I have accepted the broken and damaged part of my life as being the will of God. I still seek deliverance and ask God to fix what is damaged, but if He chooses to let them remain damaged or fix them at some other time; I will gladly glorify Him anyhow. I have to believe that God's grace is sufficient to get me through each day, even when that means I am misunderstood and not accepted, or my faith is questioned by those who do not understand: I glory in it. I found out that when you have the favor of God, you do not necessarily need the favor of man.

Undoubtedly, you will be misunderstood and perhaps talked about because you are less willing to pretend that you are whole and perfect in areas that you still have to fight, but your honesty and humility in serving God will allow God to raise you above critics. Paul said in 2 Corinthians 12:8-11, *"Three different times I begged the Lord to take it away. Each time He said, 'My gracious favor is all you need. My power works best in your weakness." So, now I am glad to boast about my weaknesses, so that the power of Christ may work through me."*

Knowing that God is working it all for His glory, I am quite content with my weaknesses, insults, hardships, persecutions, and calamities: "For when I am weak, then I am strong." I am glad to boast about my weaknesses and thank God for things that I used to complain about because they have allowed me to experience the power of God in my life. Some of the happiest persons that you will ever meet are those persons who have been through extreme afflictions. These are people who have gone through the death of loved ones, death diagnosis, rape, and divorce, but through it all the purpose of God was revealed. Others have spent their lives fighting substance abuse, being homeless or suicidal. But now God made them whole and He alone gets the glory.

These people are more likely to be the most radical, diligent worshippers because of what they have seen God do. These are people who will say, "Most gladly will I suffer," because they can witness to what their damages and brokenness have produced. Being a glad sufferer is not easy because it requires that you go beyond wanting to be comfortable more than wanting to be free. Your life might be a mess because of your suffering, but you go through it because you know what it will produce. I may have never known God the way that I do now if I wasn't given these situations to buffet me. Most gladly now will I suffer.

Never feel cheated when God doesn't fix you right away or even at all, because it means that God is producing something in you. We have to learn to be able to see God in our dreariest of circumstances. Failing to do so will result in us missing opportunities to experience God. There were some things about Jacob that had to be troubling to everybody that knew him. He was cunning, selfish, and ambitious. He felt that he had to manipulate his way into getting what God had already said He would have. Most often, this is our problem today because we think we have to force our way into places, positions, and blessings without knowing what God said we would already have. Sometimes we are fighting to take from others what God said he was going to give us.

If we ever learn how to trust God for our future, we can avoid some problems in our lives. Jacob convinces his brother Esau to give him his birthright and steals his blessing because he was not willing to trust in the will of God. His cunning acts led to his brother Esau hating him and vowing that as soon as their father died, he would kill him. Jacob's actions eventually led to him having to flee the house of his father and go to his uncle Laban's house in Haran. It was then that Jacob started having encounters with God because it was on his way there in Beersheba, that God reaffirmed the promise He had made to Abraham. Now with that going wrong in Jacob's life, and his questionable character, God makes a promise to him. Jacob said, "Surely the Lord was in the place and I knew it not." We often miss God in our lives and we do not always see what He is doing or how He is going to work, but we must trust the process.

Right in the place where Jacob's life started looking dysfunctional and out of control, God shows up looking for him. When arrived in Haran we see that the same spirit Jacob had, Laban had, also. When Jacob wanted to marry his daughter, Rachel, Laban tricks Jacob and gives him Leah. Laban cheats him out of money and does everything he could to make it difficult for him. But the hand of God was on Jacob and the blessing of his father was producing in his life. Reading this particular biblical story is how I learned that you do not have to be all that hot in order to have the favor of God rest on your life, because God chooses who He will, and blesses who He wants to bless.

When Jacob decides to return home and make peace with his brother; he has this encounter that changes him forever. Genesis, Chapter 32 begins, *"And Jacob was left alone; and there wrestled with a man with him until the breaking of day. And when he saw that he prevailed not against him, he touched the hollow of his thigh; and the hollow of Jacob's thigh was out of joint, as he wrestled with him. And he said, let me go, for the day breaketh. And he said I will not let thee go, except thou bless me. And he said unto him, "What is thy name?" And he said, Jacob. And he said, thy name shall be called no more Jacob, but Israel: for a prince has thou power with God and with men, and has prevailed."* You may be thinking at this moment, "I am Jacob," because the actions of your life may prove that something in you is damaged. Your behavior is out of control and every time you try to do what is right, things go wrong. Not only are you damaged but you have damaged others, but just like Jacob, God has not forsaken you or given up on using you, nor has He changed His mind about blessing you. There are so many things in your life that you know are not like God, and you want to fix them but they just don't come together—because you have been damaged. The greatest proof that you are Jacob is that even though you have been damaged by life, you are still here. Damaged goods, but you are here. Your being here says that God continues to bless you and that He has something He will do in you.

Leave me broken the way I am. You may view my life as being a wreck or messed up, but leave me the way I am, because if God can use me here, then He must love me everywhere. So, you can release the people that you believe have damaged you and stop making excuses for the things that have hurt you, because they're only doing their part in getting you ready for God to use you. Leave me DAMAGED.

ABOUT THE AUTHOR

Dr. Charles E. Rodgers believes that an important part of successful leadership is characterized by effective administration. He holds undergraduate degrees from Merced College in California and Indiana University in Indiana. Additionally, he holds a Master of Education (M.Ed.) from Alabama A&M University, Huntsville, Alabama, a Master of Art in Religious Education (M.A.R.E.) from Temple Baptist Seminary in Chattanooga, Tennessee, and a Doctors of Ministry in Pastoral Leadership (DMin) from Birmingham Theological Seminary.

Dr. Rodgers is the founder and Senior Pastor of Hope Community Church, a biblically based equipping fellowship located in Huntsville, Alabama. He is also the founder of the Hope Community Multipurpose Event Center, which offers banquet and conference space for community activities and engagements. He is the Executive Officer of the Greater Hope Ministerial Alliance of Churches, Inc., a fellowship of local churches called by God with the mission of servicing mankind. In addition, Dr. Rodgers has served as Honorary Chairman, Business Advisory Council on the National Congressional Committee, and is an Adjunct Professor at Birmingham Theological Seminary, Birmingham, Alabama. He is a respected and admired leader throughout the North Alabama community and respected throughout the country.

Delivered But Damaged II

Dr. Rodgers is the author of the book, *Delivered But Damaged,* an inside look at the church expectations and reality for its members. He has two additional offerings coming soon entitled *Is There Not a Cause: The Social Gospel-from Civil Rights to a Causeless People* and *Damaged but Still Dreaming.* Dr. Rodgers has over 37 years of ministry experience and has served for over 23 years in the Huntsville Community. He has effectively coached, mentored and advised many developing ministries throughout the United States.

Hope Ministries was born out of submission to the call of God. Dr. Rodgers left employment and friends in his previous stated and moved to Huntsville based on an inescapable call from God. Immediately upon arriving he began ministering to passing motorists on the streets and preaching anywhere he could find an audience. With no previous knowledge of the area, Dr. Rodgers created opportunities to share the message of the Gospel to anyone who would listen and began serving others with the resources he had available. This was the genesis of the Hope Community Church and from the first meetings attended by only six people, the church began to grow and lives began to change. Hope Community is now seen as a prototype for church growth and church planting. Now serving over 1100 members and is recognized for its structure and its ministry empowerment. The unique brand of outreach and strong appeal to young people has made Hope Community a point of reference for ministries throughout the Tennessee Valley.

In addition, it serves its members with much needed practical training, such as weekly fitness classes; financial fitness training; and Credit Training and Budgeting, weekly training for youth and tutoring; all of which is open to the greater community. Hope Community Church has been among the leading organizations in the Tennessee Valley in the area of social action; providing food, clothing and other essential services to the needy residence in our area. Dr. Rodgers spearheaded a team that ministers to the homeless encampments; provides food, blankets essential toiletries and transportation to those finding themselves in these unfortunate settings. Through his vision, Hope Community has been able to acquire several houses in the area and has allowed needy families to live in them without cost. Dr. Rodgers also initiated a partnership with local city schools to sponsor certain teachers with supplies and underprivileged students with coats and food support. Hope Community Church offers advance learning through its childcare services, Hope Christian Daycare (HCD). HCD offers compassionate services, as well as a learning based program using the Abeka curriculum. Hope Christian Daycare has serviced this community for over 20 years with a strong emphasis toward student achievement. Dr. Rodgers is also the founder and Chief Executive of the Hope Prep Academy, a private academy specializing in math and sciences. The aim of the Kindergarten to third grade school is to provide an advanced and challenging curriculum to children who would otherwise not be able to access it. Hope Prep Academy has provided tuition free education to half its student population and reduced tuition to many others through scholarships from donors. Dr. Rodgers is active in many causes and has served in many community based groups and organizations. He currently serves as a member and former Vice-President of the Greater Huntsville Interdenominational Ministerial Fellowship, a member of North Huntsville Community United for Action (NHCUA), a community leadership group for minority rights in the Huntsville area where he served as the Chairman of the Economic Empowerment Group. Dr. Rodgers has been active in Stop the Violence Campaigns through organizing marches, door to door engagements, to sponsoring a Stop the Violence Rap concert that attracted over 30 acts to support the cause.

The many ministries and services that Hope Community Church offers through the vision of Dr. Rodgers are truly a miracle and blessing for many. Dr. Rodgers' love for his congregation and his community is displayed by the attentiveness to the things he does. He and Lady Carlett Rodgers have been married for over 34 years and have two children (Tiffani and Ryan) and nine grandchildren.

Dr. Charles Rodgers